Introduction

I have written this book on beha peace time part time soldiers, who like m their spare time over the years.

There are many memoirs about war time soldiering explaining in great details the rigours of combat and being away from home for long periods of time, but there are actually very few about the Territorial Army, its shoestring budgets and sudden changes of plan, the bonds of friendship that once forged, last a lifetime.

The stockbroker's, lorry drivers, gardeners and chief executives who when together have a common theme. Some of these individuals have gone on to be successful businessmen and some have had hard times but you can always pick up a conversation exactly where you left it twelve years before.

We are unusual citizens; we have had two lives and because of this we are all much more rounded individuals and have a sense of camaraderie which civilians fail to grasp. You only get to know someone when you have experienced being wet and cold and extremes of fear and exhilaration.

To all the Territorial Army and Army Reserve soldiers, both male and female, past present and future, I salute you!

John Bennett June 2016 (amended 2021)

Foreword.

The Army Reserve was created as the Territorial Force in 1908 by the Secretary of State for War, Richard Haldane, when the Territorial and Reserve Forces Act 1907 combined the previously civilian-administered Volunteer Force, with the mounted Yeomanry. Its original purpose was home defence, although the establishment of the Territorial and Army Volunteer Reserve in 1967 involved a restructuring and revised doctrine leading to the provision of routine support for the Regular Army overseas.

Millions of citizens have served as Cold War Warriors over the last century. It has never ceased to amaze me what our volunteer servicemen and women have done, and continue to do, for their country and their comrades. Their selfless commitment, all the time juggling work / family / other interests; in the line of duty are a reminder to us all. As Winston Churchill once said: 'the Reservist is twice the citizen'. I and many others are immensely proud of all of their achievements and grateful for their service.

One of those stories is recounted here, by John Bennett, who in 1977 walked through the TA Centre gates to begin an outstanding part time, paid career in the then Territorial Army (now the Army Reserve). He worked his way through the ranks, ending up with almost of 30 years' service, as a Major in the 3rd Battalion, The Princess of Wales's Royal Regiment. But, it didn't stop there and he completed his uniformed service with the cadets in the rank of Lieutenant Colonel.

During his illustrious career I had the pleasure of serving alongside him, also on operations in Kosovo, when we visited our 1st Battalion. He recounts a selection of stories taken from during his service – the highs and the lows. What struck me about John was his dedication to service, his selfless commitment to bringing out the best in others and the comradeship with others.

I commend John Bennett for his diligence in replaying the stories taken from his service and for his continued work with the PWRR Regimental Association, the Regimental Museum in Dover and also the Regimental Heritage Committee – 'twice the citizen'!

COL JAP LADD TD VR
Col INFANTRY Reserves

Index

Preface

Dawn began to dilute the shadows on the trees and the smells all around become more intense. The autumn chill produces dew drops on the spider webs. The senses become heightened, every leaf movement, every bird flying by sounds intense. It seems ages ago we left our comfortable trenches, complete with sleeping compartment and a warm brew to hand.

Having walked miles and dug in hurriedly, we lie together in silence, listening for the sound of approaching armour, looking for the signs that would alert us to infantry approaching through the woods. Thumbs rubbing the safety catch glancing at the range card whilst instinctively measuring the distance to the bushes on the right of arc.

There are no startled birds, no escaping animals, so for the moment we feel safe. Wait, a noise off to our right, everyone becomes tense and the click of safety catches being gently released.

A gentle whistling gets louder and from along the track, a figure can be made out walking along just in front of us. We all relax and the adrenaline drains, it's a hiker out to the take in the early morning air.

A German gentleman in his early 60s looking for all the world if he had just come from the Bier Keller, dressed in his lederhosen, pointed hat and walking boots, and the customary walking stick that the local hikers use.

We know this area well, every year we deploy from Dover, a mammoth two-day drive and immediately deploy to the same woods as last year and dig in. Our Brigade has already been exercising for a week, so we would slip in seamlessly during a planned lull.

How the mind wanders, this was forty plus years ago. Now I sit in my comfortable hide waiting for the deer to emerge from the wood line to get a photograph. The senses are still the same; the woods still look as they did then, nothing has changed.

The training completed way back then was to prepare us for war which if it had happened, would have been over so fast, I am sure we would be passing the Soviets at Dover docks going in the other direction.

For a Cold War Warrior to have lived through the last twenty years of the might of the USSR, was a unique experience.

The training was hard and intensive, 6 Field Force, our master and administrative hub, treated us as equals. Helicopters, Hercules transport aircraft were never a problem during these tense times.

It was not uncommon to be collected from a regional airport on a Friday night, and flown to Thetford for weekend training and be returned late Sunday evening. The defence budget was about 4% of GDP and we had all the hardware we needed.

Our clothing and personal equipment was very basic, having not changed much since the late 1960s. Waterproof jackets were not available until 1983 and then they were only showerproof.

I would like to reflect on my time serving my country and having a ball!

Chapter 1.

The early beginnings

At the end of the Second World War the 21st Army group under General Bernard Montgomery, was ordered to occupy the ground they were holding and prepare to be an army of occupation.

The British Army of the Rhine was formed on 25 August 1945 from the British Liberation Army. Its original function was to control the corps districts which were running the military government of the British zone of occupied Germany. After the assumption of government by civilians, it became the command formation for the troops in Germany only, rather than being responsible for administration as well.

As the potential threat of Soviet invasion across the North German Plain into West Germany increased, BAOR became more responsible for the defence of West Germany than its occupation.

It became the primary formation controlling the British contribution to NATO after the formation of the alliance in 1949. Its primary combat formation was British I Corps. From 1952, the commander-in-chief of the BAOR was also the commander of NATO's Northern Army Group (NORTHAG), in the event of a general war with the Soviet Union and the Warsaw Pact.

BAOR had tactical nuclear weapons capability. In 1967, the standing force was reduced in strength to 53,000 troops. the force in BAOR became reliant on reinforcement troops being deployed from the UK.

The reality of this was to provide a blocking force to slow down the Soviet advance. This was to enable the politicians to make the relevant decisions in conjunction with our allies, to deploy the battlefield nuclear weapons.

I was recruited by a friend of mine in the village, Tony Young back in 1977, who suggested if I joined the mechanical transport platoon, I would get a HGV3 driving licence in about a year. This was very appealing as I could then drive the recovery vehicle at work and get a pay rise.

I visited the barracks and was told that because I was a mechanic, I would be posted to the REME. This seemed like a busman's holiday, so I declined to sign on the dotted line. I wanted to get away from fixing things and being a driver was a perfect change.

I went back the following summer and signed on in the July and was told I could do my recruit course in September which was fine, but I became very excited when advised that it would be in Germany!

I received no military training at all during the run up to the camp in Germany except for a day on the ranges where I did some shooting. I had fired the .303 rifle in the cadets, but this big black thing with a kick like a mule was something to be reckoned with.

The self-loading rifle was the current weapon of the infantry at this time, the older versions had a wooden butt and stock but the later ones were black plastic furniture. I had a good score and guys were talking about being on the shooting team which sounded quite fun, but my MT sergeant, Terry Fry put the dampener on the idea and told the others I was needed as a driver.

I secretly was happy with this as I had found out my allocated personal weapon was the sub machine gun, a very light weapon easily wrapped in plastic and hidden in the cab of a land rover. More comfortable on the shoulder, the SLR rifle did leave you with a bruised shoulder for days.

The ranges we fired on were called Lydden Spout, an area just behind Shakespeare cliff in Dover; it was very quiet and secluded. It was a fantastic day in August and incredibly hot. The brand-new hairy shirt was the only dampener on the day, my goodness do they scratch your skin, they only become bearable after 3000 washes, and a shave with a razor around the collar. On balance though more comfortable than the old battledress I wore when I was a cadet. The ranges have long since gone and the A20 runs through there now.

As you leave Dover heading towards Ashford, there is a turning to the Samphire Hoe nature reserve. Immediately behind this are the remains of the old range butts, if you had never seen them in their heyday, they just look like mounds of earth but they make me smile and think on a simpler time long ago.

The uniform we were issued with was quite heavy, double lined which retained the rain. It was perfect for the cold weather, but useless in the rain and during the summer months.

The jumper was very warm but as I alluded to previously, but as I alluded to earlier, the shirts were awful. We had a pair of lightweight denims which were comfortable which pressed into great creases. After a while you realised that you could sew the creases in to save ironing time.

The boots were short and quite comfortable when worn in. We also had puttees; they were a throwback from a time long ago! I was advised to wear the boots to work to get them comfortable for the exercise in Germany. This paid dividends and avoided blisters in due course.

I envisaged I would fly to Germany with the rest of the recruits and the battalion, but as a driver, you had to drive soldier qualified or not! On the first day we left in convoy and drove to Harwich. The best description of this would be slow and tedious, but even that was pushing it. With rest breaks it took seven hours, in my car it would have been just over three!

We caught the overnight ferry to Esbjerg in Denmark and then drove down to the exercise area in Schleswig-Holstein in Northern Germany. The field camp was sparse and as we arrived, it started to rain which lasted the whole of the first week.

My memories of that week are minimal, a blur as it went so fast, we learned about weapons, tactics and how to live in the field. The rain was annoying but we learned to live with it. On the Saturday we had a day off and went to Hamburg for sightseeing and beer, but had to be back to camp early as we were joining the NATO exercise first thing Sunday morning.

When we awoke the rain had finally stopped, everywhere smelt damp and our kit was steaming in the early September sun.

I joined 10 platoon which back then was based in Canterbury. It was an infantry platoon on permanent loan from C company in Hastings, to give the specialists a full grounding in infantry tactics before we joined our specialist platoons. I knew some of the guys who were in my platoon, as I had met them back in Canterbury. We loaded our kit then deployed with C company in the back of 3 tonne trucks.

I didn't really know the guys in the platoon well, but they were a really diverse bunch of guys. The platoon sergeant was called Frank Hill. Frank had recently joined our battalion from the Royal Green Jackets after his 22 years of regular service and had settled in Sittingbourne.

He was a very good platoon sergeant who looked after the platoon extremely well, he would always appear at the moment you felt miserable wet and cold for a chat and morale boost.

The section corporal was Mick Page, a carpenter who lived in Ashford. He was a real character, a true London boy, very efficient and font of all knowledge both legitimate and a little dubious!

No matter how dirty and cold you were after days lying in the mud, Mick would always be immaculately dressed and clean. Even camouflage cream seemed an art for Mick. He went on to be a Regimental policeman, the epitome of the poacher turned game keeper; he was perfect for the job. A lifelong friend to this day!

Paul Barker came from Sittingbourne and worked in the local paper mill in administration he was the section second in command, Paul had joined the army quite late in life, and then he was in his early thirties I believe. If he had joined earlier, he would have certainly been an officer.

Paul had wisdom and experience that others only aspired to. He always had the correct solution to the problems and in later times I served with him in the MT platoon and enjoyed my time with him immensely.

Jim Dew lived in Ashford and worked for The British Rail Engineering works in Ashford, now long closed, was in my section, Jim was a great laugh and I served with him later in my career in the Signals platoon.

Jim went on to work for Ford Motor company in a management role and subsequently for Jaguar. A very clever guy, his service with us was cut short when he had to move house to take a job promotion. He transferred to the Royal Anglian Regiment, but they were a home defence battalion and Jim felt they were never quite like the NATO role TA battalion he had just left.

Kelvin Rushton from Aylesham was known as Willie after the television personality of that era, he used to dine out on stories of actually being related to the great man but it transpired he was exaggerating the truth a little!

Initially we were held in reserve which meant other than a bit of patrolling and statutory guard duties, we had a couple of days to settle in.

I was paired up with a guy called Harrison whose Christian name I forget. He came from our sister battalion in Horsham and was from North London. He had joined earlier in the year and had more military experience than me, but I found it quite amusing he was going to be a chef on completion of his training.

We dug a good two-man trench in the forest with excellent overhead cover; this was supported with logs that had been found around the area. In the covered area we dug out storage areas in the sandy soil for our kit and mess tins, and it became home from home.

The covered area enabled us to be able to sleep comfortably in sleeping bags the guard duties were spread out so we only had to do one hour a night. The woods were home to several species of owl which were very vocal after dusk.

At quiet times the local red squirrel population busied themselves feeding on the packets of nuts and raisins issued in the twenty-four-hour ration packs. Oh, for a digital camera, there were some fantastic shots.

My first experience of sleeping in one of the enormous forests which cover Northern Germany was a sensation of peace and tranquillity, the freedom of that first experience was never quite the same again. Probably the best sleep I have ever had.

We were replenished after dark every night by the company quartermaster sergeant. He brought water and rations and goodies from the local shops which were very welcome.

One night he came with the chefs and fresh rations, freshly cooked stewed steak casserole, with boiled potato and as much cabbage as we could fit into our mess tin. The chefs had excelled themselves and we had a dessert as well. This was sponge pudding and hot custard. We thought this was great but it was a precursor for a very hard night to come.

The whole platoon was briefed and we moved out in silence and walked for three hours and set an ambush along a well-used track. The enemy reconnaissance units had been spotted using this route the previous night, and our mission was to capture some of the enemy. We laid in complete silence for two hours, shivering quietly, totally unable to move. The clouds parted and owls began to call to each other.

I thought I was dreaming when I saw a huge stag on the track just a few yards away. I didn't hear it coming and a blink in an eye it vanished as quickly as it appeared. Just before dawn we withdrew back about a kilometre, and after a few minutes we heard trucks approaching. At last transport home to our holes!

The next day we were briefed that we were going to be the blocking force to cover a divisional withdrawal. We were reinforced by a further section of guys from another company; they had 2-inch mortars with illuminated rounds. They also had a general-purpose machine gun which was new to me.

The main road was two hundred meters to our front and at the appointed time the rumbling of tanks and the associated vehicles starting to pass by. The noise became much louder as the tracked vehicles passed. The forest shook and trees started to fall around us. We were told to stay in our trenches for safety, but after five hours the ground was moving. An armoured divisional move involved hundreds of vehicles, and the sound of this road move went on for most of the night.

The soil was basically sand and the vibration of the armour turned the ground around us into a quicksand. Our hard dug and fitted out trenches gradually started to collapse, we had to pack up our kit and then move back a kilometre for safety. In the morning we heard that a large enemy force attacked our position but didn't see a soul.

The umpires were confused as we had been there when they came around earlier that day. We heard the attack and the gunfire but didn't react to it. We heard that the local police had closed the road after the tanks passed as it had collapsed in the area around where we were dug in.

The whole company packed their kit and withdrew on foot westwards, after an hour of so moving in a tactical formation through the rides in the woods, we came upon a clearing where the vehicles and more importantly, a hot meal was waiting.

After a couple of hours rest the company moved out on the vehicles but this time it was a short move to wooded hillside. We dug in again but this time the ground was hard and full of roots and stones. This took hours and was by no means up to the standard of the previous attempt. The wood overlooked a rolling grass covered valley, and after several days of murky and wet weather, the sun came out and it seemed a very pleasant place to be.

You could see for several kilometres from this position, one of the lectures we received during the basic training phase was the importance of always digging in to protect yourself from the threat of artillery barrage.

The might of the Soviet artillery was such, that a divisional barrage could obliterate a whole square kilometre in less than 3 minutes! We all took an involuntary swallow at that point. Looking to my front whilst laying in this still and silent position, I worked out what a square kilometre looked like and thought of the devastation. Mental note to oneself: always dig a deep hole and reinforce with overhead protection.

The 'enemy force' consisted of German armour which I had never seen before; the tanks were Leopard 1s which even by today's standards are quite formidable.

During the afternoon the low rumble of the tanks was heard. These appeared in the ground immediately in front of us moving across our front. They were accompanied by MARDER, an armoured vehicle designed to carry infantry, so clearly, we were going to get some business shortly.

A group of umpires appeared and after throwing a couple of thunder flashes we were deemed all dead and had to remain in position for three hours before re-joining the battle.

The disappointment of not engaging this enemy was overwhelmed by the fact I couldn't remember how long ago I actually managed to get two hours sleep, so after a quick brew of tea, the sleeping bag came out and silence descended over our position. The umpires woke us up after just over three hours, to advise we were to prepare for an attack.

At dusk the enemy approached up and a massive eruption of small arms fire, machine gun and thunder flashes exploded and after a few minutes the umpires called a halt and decreed we have destroyed the enemy.

We had no anti-tank weapons and no immediate mortar or artillery support so I am not sure how we were supposed to have destroyed the armour? The enemy then rested and brewed up allowing us to have a good look inside their vehicles and inspect the weaponry they used.

As midnight approached, we filled in our trenches and pulled back about a kilometre where the trucks were waiting. A six-hour road move followed. Day and night blend into one when you are living in the field, time seems to have its own rhythm. We had worked out it was Friday morning; it only seemed like a few days since leaving camp.

When we returned back to camp, I experienced for the first time the 'end of exercise' big breakfast. Subsequently over the years I had so many of these but the first one invokes exciting memories.

We lined up our kit and weapons on the floor and queued up with both mess tins and mug and we could not believe what we were given. Two slices of fried bread placed in the bottom of the large mess tin with two rashers of greasy slimy bacon.
Tinned sausages followed and even today I yearn for these, you can still get them crushed together in a 15oz can, filled with lard, heaven in a tin! You could have up to four sausages!

Next was a concoction of left overs, from the rear party supper the night before, probably fried onions with peppers, mushrooms and whatever else had been on the menu in camp over the previous couple of days. Next came the beans, a whole ladle full, by now the mess tin resembled a small hill! Finally, two fried eggs were gently placed on top. If you were lucky there was sliced German sausage as well.

The small mess tin had a generous dollop of porridge and finally a big mug of strong tea. In the ration packs were chocolate bars and oatmeal blocks, these were squirreled away for future use, after all they had been in the ration pack tins for years surely, they would last a couple of weeks in my combat jacket pocket. We could have as many as we wanted.

The quartermaster had arranged for a mobile shower unit to be in camp for our return, these were based on a 4-ton truck with the capacity to heat water to lukewarm and piped into a tent through copper pipes with a shower head every metre. It was a glorious experience, the first proper wash in days, clean clothes and dry boots. The smell of deodorant covered the smell of dank rancid clothing which an hour ago permeated the area.

We just had time to pack up our personal kit and a couple of bottles of Herforder Pils and get some sleep ready to return home.

The journey was made in reverse order but the weather in the North Sea had been so bad over the previous few days the ferries were out of sequence. We sat in the docks for hours, thankful for the rather large packed lunch we had been provided and the chocolate and oatmeal blocks, we had hidden away.

The crossing was awful, eighteen hours back to Harwich and home to Canterbury at one in the morning on the Monday morning before starting work at 8am!

Our battalion was fully manned during this period; we had been up scaled to the same amount of equipment and personal as a similar sized regular battalion. We had 650 officers and soldiers during this time. There were twelve rifle company platoons, an 81mm mortar platoon. One of the barrels could be traced back to the Korean war from its barrel record, showing how many rounds it had fired, and an anti-tank Platoon.

When I just joined, they were issued with the 120mm Wombat but latterly it was MILAN, a French made wire guided missile, extremely accurate and very effective. We had a platoon of assault pioneers, these guys were in house engineers, and they blew up things and set wire obstacles in front of the company positions. We also had a reconnaissance platoon taken from the very best soldiers in the battalion.

Chapter 2

Whoops it wasn't my fault!

During the year following the return from the first camp, I trained to get my HGV licence. This was undertaken by Tony who was a qualified driving instructor in the old 1960s Bedford RL, although we were fully manned and had all the support kit, it was primarily cast offs when the regular units received brand new kit.

These vehicles were a prime example of this. Our fleet was quite reliable but getting spare parts to keep them going was sometimes challenging. These old bits of kit were well built with a six-cylinder petrol engine and solid 16-gauge steel front bumpers.

Very useful when being cut up in London by a brand-new Rover 800. The bumper had a slight paint discolouration but the Rover needed a new rear quarter panel!

The RL was quite good fun to drive but hard work in traffic. The gears did have synchromesh but this was worn out on most of the trucks. You had to drive as if there was none present; this meant dipping the clutch twice to get the gears in and out, no fun when under load towing a heavy trailer!

On a straight road with a bit of weight in the back on a gentle downward slope you could get 75mph of these relics, pure wind noise from the drop-down windows, the cross-country tyres howling and enough vibration to give you white knuckle syndrome!

Our main training areas used were either Thetford in Norfolk or down at Aldershot. This was years before the M25 so all the journeys were by A roads, a very tiring experience after a gruelling week at work.

After I passed my test, I went into see my manager at work with the intention of showing him my test pass certificate and hinting that now I could drive the recovery vehicle I perhaps should earn a little more money. Before I could speak, he said that because I showed an interest in driving the recovery trucks the company were going to put me through an HGV class 1 licence at no cost to myself.

He said arrange a provisional licence and they would get me on the first available course. When I showed him my licence (hiding the HGV Class 3 pass certificate!) he made a call and I was on a week's training the following Monday morning. Within ten days, I had passed two HGV tests and received a £1.50 per hour pay rise! Thank you everyone!

In the run up to annual camp in 1979 we attended quite a few training exercises at company, battalion and at brigade level, this year we were not attending the exercises in Germany as we were deemed to be in the training cycle of training/operations which could be done in the UK on one of several large training areas.

We were going to deploy to Okehampton camp on Dartmoor. A UK road move to a training camp differs slightly in as much that the costs are borne by the MOD from the UK training budget, a fraction of the training budget of BAOR and as a result a certain number of cutbacks befall all TA units.

One should also note we were approaching a moratorium which post annual camp, hit the TA units quite hard but I will come onto that further on.

One Thursday night our MTO Derek called all the drivers into the office and briefed us of how we intended to get the whole battalion to Devon, a total of 320 miles from Canterbury! He outlined rest stops, refuelling arrangements and how our first few days would be spent supporting the battalion's range packages.

One of the guys suggested that the troops would be in the back of the trucks for a rather long time and to all our surprise Derek said a 'Troop train' would be transporting the soldiers.

It turned out that the train was a relic from WW2. The carriages were attached to a modern locomotive but they had minimal facilities. The seats were wooden benches, no heating; windows jammed shut from the passage of time and a single toilet per carriage. I am told when you lifted the lid on the toilet the tracks were visible underneath! No health and safety in 1979!

This was in fact the last ever UK troop movement by train using these ancient carriages, now I assume they are now tucked away at the back of a railway museum.

The road party deployed very early on the Saturday morning after assembling at our respective TA centres around 19:30 the previous evening. We loaded the vehicles, put the weapons in transportation bundles and were ready to go at 06:00. We dropped the non-drivers with their kit to the goods yard at Canterbury West station and headed westward.

It was a long and uneventful journey; we refuelled at Bulford using the facilities of the 1st Battalion and had a meal in their cookhouse. We changed drivers every hour and finally we arrived at Okehampton at four pm. After unloading quickly, we had evening meal at 19:00 but our day was not finished yet. If we felt tired and road weary it was nothing compared to the guys on the train.

I discovered during the evening that all the companies had dropped their soldiers at their local stations very early that morning before continuing by road as we had done.

The troop train had been positioned at Ramsgate goods yard overnight and the first troops from B company started their day at 05:30 meandering their way to Okehampton via Canterbury, Dover and Folkestone to collect their Platoons.

They then went on to Hastings to collect C company and onwards to Maidstone, Tonbridge and Sevenoaks to collect E company then finally Guildford for A company. The train then went direct to Okehampton to a siding just below the station which looked as if it hadn't been used since the days of Dr Beeching!

We took the trucks down to the siding at 22:00 and the train arrived at 22:15 with the most tired and saddle sore soldiers I have ever seen hobbling about! At the end of camp, we did the same thing in reverse!

The whole battalion was up and having breakfast by 06:00, quite a feat considering the day we had all had previously. Credit however goes to the handful of chefs we had. Not only had they prepared the road party a huge meal at 19:00 the previous night, they also excelled themselves by feeding the rail party at 23:00.

Somewhere in between they had some sleep because they were up again at 04:00 to cook breakfast for everyone. These guys were a disparate bunch, Jack Turner from C company, an irascible chap who worked 120% for his guys on company weekends, Brian 'The Weasel' Stevens from HQ company in Canterbury who delivered a cracking meal but you probably wouldn't want to watch him cook it or your appetite might wane!

There was Doug Stapley known by all as Staples, his reputation for being excused shorts was widely known across the battalion. He was an ex regular Royal Artillery corporal who had reached his age ceiling as the recruiting sergeant at forty-five and rebadged as Army Catering Corps for another ten years!

Staples was trained as a butcher in civilian street, but was a dab hand at breakfasts. These characters plus many more that came and went were the core guys in the kitchen during those early years.

The whole battalion deployed on a range package to the ranges behind the camp on Dartmoor. The drivers usually were not involved so I became used to the free time (when it was not raining) to do some bird watching and take in the glorious views across Dartmoor. This was not to be my last time here.

On the third day of the ranges the Regimental Sergeant Major caught me lurking and decided I should assist with the range team. It was sunny and warm so of course I agreed to help.

My task was to pull the cord on the 'effects gun' to initiate the firing. It was to simulate enemy firing back at the soldiers actually they were quite effective. The effects gun has a 30-round magazine which contained 7.62mm blank ammunition. It looked roughly like one of the old WW2 sten guns except they had a short barrel and a tripod.

The whole unit in its assembled state was only nine inches tall. It was fired by a trigger attached to a thin dark green wire. This gun was set out near the targets and the cable carefully laid so the troops couldn't see it.

My role was to walk down the range with the range staff and as they passed the end of the wire my job was to pick up the cable and tug furiously making the gun fire three ten round bursts. The soldiers then engaged the targets and carried with the range package.

It was during one of these run downs that the machine gunner to my right hit the ground just a few inches away from me and immediately fired a couple of long bursts. The ringing in my years lasted months and now at my senior age I have tinnitus and reduced hearing in my right ear, probably attributed to this.

I did this repeatedly all day and was having quite good fun, as I got better at getting ten rounds off at a time so I became a little cocky, on the final time, the last ten rounds were left. With a big flourish I tugged the cable too hard and the effects gun leapt up into the air – just as a machine gun to my left opened up and shot the effects gun into small pieces.

Oh, dear was I in the poop. The effects gun was supplied by the ranges and this was the last working one they had. Apparently, they should have been consigned to museums years before but there was nothing similar to replace them.

When we returned the parts to the range stores there was uproar, how did we do it? Did we leave the gun in full view? I said the cable became stuck on a large piece of granite in a V groove, and when I pulled a little harder the whole lot jumped into the air and the accident happened. This was begrudging accepted and I vowed not to be cocky in the future.

The next day I was back bird watching and reading my book. My colleague then had to accompany the range team and when the correct place came on the range, he was given the nod and he had to yell 'Bang Bang Bang' at the top of his voice! Glad I didn't have to do that!

The next day I drove B company to the submachine gun range. This was my personal weapon but although I carried it everywhere when we deployed, I had never fired it. Before the soldiers were ready to start the guy, who was running the range asked if the drivers would like to have a go.

We of course we up for it and very soon we were standing on the firing point being briefed. It was an interesting weapon; it had a folding stock, designed to fire from a vehicle cab or in close confines. You were never allowed to fire it on automatic, because the SMG was so light and had a short barrel, it was deemed dangerous.

The safety catch lever had three settings, first position up was safety, second was single shot and the third was fully automatic. In the third position it kept firing until you released the trigger.

We had a full magazine of ammunition, the gun fired 9mm parabellum, and the range of the weapon was one hundred meters at the most certainly, and not accurate. The range conducting officer said, 'twenty rounds grouping in your own time carry on' I took aim, clicked the switch to single shot and squeezed the trigger.... After the first shot I released the trigger and the gun kept firing, full auto!

I had to hang onto it for grim death, the conducting office shouted stop! I told him it was doing it all by itself! Loads of hollering shouting and guys taking cover. Finally, it stopped and I looked at the switch and it was still on single shot. Despite protesting my innocence my pleas were ignored and I was placed on a charge!

I gave the weapon back to its owner and sat in the truck grumbling to anyone who would listen. The next guys lined up on the range, ten of them in a straight line. The range conducting officer said the commands and the guys opened fire. The same happened to all of them; they emptied their magazines exactly as I had done.

The range officer went red and started shouting questioning the guy's birth rights and parentage suggesting they were stitching him up. The warden came over and closed the ranges as we were definitely not allowed to fire on automatic. Off we went back to camp and I was called up in front of the RSM.

He had witnessed the events with the effects gun the day before so my card was already marked. He took great delight in fashioning me a new rear hole, all the time I was standing to attention bricking myself. I was then marched to the company commander who then improved on the RSM's best efforts.

I had ruined the range, guys were unable to fire their range course, oh dear naughty boy etc etc... £150 fine and three days in the guardroom!

After twenty-four hours, and all the time moving at the double with the duty nco yelling in my ear, I was called into the RSM's office (still doubling) gosh I was knackered! The taste of humble pie must have been bitter. It would appear that the MOD had bought a large batch of 9mm ammunition from Pakistan very cheaply.

The charge loaded into the rounds was below the specification needed to throw the SMG and pistol's working parts far enough back to click the trigger catch into place, hence the automatic effect! I was not happy when it happened to me but I would have been really uncomfortable if it had been all thirteen rounds in the pistol!

I had all the cushy jobs after that but although the charge was wiped from the records, the fine; once it had been put on the books had to be refunded after camp. It took eight months to get the money back!

The worst part of the two-week camp was on the day off. After breakfast on the Saturday morning, we cadged a lift into the local town of Okehampton. It was a small market town having been established for centuries as a base for the farming communities. The main road through the town widened in the centre for the market back in the day. We wandered about the town, had coffee in a cafe and generally chilled out.

We missed the lunchtime transport back as we were queuing at the chip shop. We could either walk the two miles back to camp up a 45-degree road, or wait until 11pm for the next run back.

During the afternoon we went to the pub nearest the centre of town and had a local beer. The locals were a grumpy old bunch of yokels, they were drinking pints of scrumpy, and this was a rough cider, dark, with recently deceased things floating in it with a kick like a mule but with a taste of sweet apples.

We sat in the pub for a couple of hours playing table skittles and darts, all the time the locals glared at us whilst still drinking pints of the nasty stuff. One of them suggested we try some with some smirking and tittering. Being the macho sort, we obviously could take some of this stuff.

The landlord refused to serve us pints; he said only halves for the first timers as it was lethal stuff. The yokels had had about five pints each and it wasn't even four pm so what could possibly go wrong....... It was lovely and at 10:30 pm I felt as silly as a sheep, managed to get the transport back to camp.

That night I was convinced I was floating six inches above bed, the weirdest sensation. I vowed I wouldn't drink it ever again, well not until the next time we visited Okehampton!

Sunday morning started slowly with a church service at 10:00 which I just made. After lunch we packed the vehicles ready to deploy on a four-day exercise. I was not feeling too well and didn't really participate fully.

I didn't get the joke when the arms kote store man handed me an SLR rifle for the exercise, muttering something about not being trustworthy enough to have an SMG, very funny! I vowed I would never drink again.

Memories of this week were fuzzy, and before I knew it, we were on the way home.

Chapter 3

The Defence Moratorium

The UK government had overspent the budget for defence in 1979, and just after we returned from Okehampton, we were faced with stringent cuts. The miners' strike and the three-day week, had made a huge dent into the UK's financial pot, and this needed to be clawed back as a matter of urgency.

You could only train if you weren't being paid known as C1 training, everything was cancelled. The paper for typing on, envelopes for posting them were just not available.

All resources were focussed on the Northern Ireland operation, maintaining our NATO commitment and Germany and of course the United Nations tasks were already committed to.

A call for extreme husbandry of resources was put out service wide. The TA took the brunt of these cuts and life pretty much ground to a halt. The permanent staff suffered too, they could drive about in the week to support weekend training, attending meetings and moving stores around so the soldiers could be properly supported, when the fuel embargo set in the weekly conferences had to be done by telephone, and even the CO couldn't use his staff car!

The supply of spare parts ceased and because we had old and unreliable vehicles, they became unroadworthy and unusable very quickly. The practise of 'cannibalising' vehicles could not be used in peacetime, but resourceful unit mechanics used to 'find' working parts from vehicles already broken. If a repair took longer than four hours to complete it was sent to a base repair workshop where more in depth action could be taken.

Questions would eventually be asked when a vehicle was sent to workshops to have a clutch fitted and during the final test, they would find that brake units, carburettors, water pumps and alternators would have failed at the same time!

One anomaly of the workshop system was many of the civilian staff working there would be TA mechanic's during the drill night or weekends, many of them culpable of the parts switching. I was witness to a conversation between the workshop and our quartermaster trying to work out why a £50 in value job would render the vehicle uneconomical to repair?

We all did it, there was always a 'sacrificial lamb' usually the oldest and least reliable vehicle held on charge. It took years to catch up with the vehicle repairs.

There were no twenty-four-hour ration packs for training so you couldn't be fed, no ammunition nor were training areas available. The world stopped completely until the next financial year came around.

Being resourceful, some company quartermaster sergeants have a stash of ration packs which were for 'emergencies' not on the books and the quartermaster didn't know about them. This at least managed to get the guys together for low level training occasionally. The whip round for the 'chip shop run' was common place such was the eagerness and loyalty of the TA soldier to train.

The sound of our guys running about doing section attacks whilst yelling bang bang was hilarious! The funniest thing I heard during these difficult times, was a section commander telling off his section gunner about wasting ammunition, and that by firing his machine gun in three to five rounds bursts provided more effective and accurate fire.

The poor guy had been running about on full auto, that is to say he kept saying bang bang bang bang bang etc, instead of just shouting bang bang bang! This was so ludicrous but at that time these strange events were the norm.

One day the permanent staff discovered a hidden stash of 7.62 blank rounds in links, used for the general-purpose machine guns. Enough ration packs to feed the company for a week and a complete C42 radio from the pre-Clansmen days, in full working order. The ingenuity of the TA soldier was at worst almost illegal but at best, the TA scrounger was compared to his regular counterparts in a league of their own!

Recruiting suffered as well during this time, the TA recruit courses were reduced in frequency and after a couple of months the guys leaving were more frequent than those joining. This effect took years to be addressed despite some very active and professional guys working hard at the task.

Our training major during this time had to use a land rover to visit the outstations and plan and reconnoitre training areas. He would normally use the estate car we were issued with, but true to form the way it was accounted for made it impossible to use it due to the mileage constraints imposed on the use of what they deem as 'White fleet' albeit red in colour.

Consequently, I arrived early for training one Thursday night, to be asked to go out with a jack and change the wheel of the training major's land rover a couple of miles out of town. This wasn't a problem so off I went.

I duly found him by the side of the road and attended to the flat tyre. I was just underneath the land rover pulling out some wire wrapped around the axle, and heard movement above my head.

As I emerged liquid was cascading down all over me. As I looked up there were 3 sheep looking down at me from over the tailboard! The training major had received permission to graze his sheep on the grass area behind our garages, as there was no petrol allocation for the contractors and the grass was getting out of hand. He had neglected to tell me they were there. I was a little smelly for the rest of the evening!

Chapter 4

A very sad day

Over my twenty-seven years I enjoyed myself immensely but on one occasion back in the early 1980s I had a rude awakening. Every year in early August we supported the annual Buffs Sunday reunion by providing a guard on the Cathedral parade and then organising the food and the reunion hosting back at the barracks.

This particular year it was a really hot August and the turnout was above average, there were hundreds of veterans milling around and having a great time.

I was driving this year so my friend had a drink and I would drive us home. The day was fantastic; the marching guard from HQ company was nearly 70 strong, all in our No2 dress and highly polished boots. We had a curry for lunch which went down well. We circulated with the Buffs veterans listening to their war stories. Many of these characters were WW2 and Korea veterans so their stories of real combat were fascinating to us. At around four pm we decided to head off home.

The next day I received a call at work to advise that one of the guys in our group I had been drinking with, had been involved in a car crash and sadly died. He had been drinking and the assumption was he had fallen asleep.

My friend Tony and I were picked as pall bearers which we were really upset about. Practising the drills took time and when the day came, we did him proud in front of his grieving family.

There was a sense of guilt as perhaps we could have influenced him if we had stayed longer. The powers that be knew we had been together prior to him leaving, so it seemed to us as if we being taught a lesson, indeed a hard one, to take given the circumstances.

Because of the loss there was a vacancy within the platoon for a lance corporal. I was duly promoted and as always, I arrived at the TA centre, not read the orders and fell in to parade.

I was told I was incorrectly dressed and should report to the colour sergeant in the stores to collect a stripe. This I duly did and Andy the quartermaster sergeant in his usual helpful manner searched everywhere for one.

He eventually opened a dustbin sack and removed a shirt. He then began to remove a stripe with a pair of scissors. As he did this it dawned on me what he was doing.

The shirt had blood stains on it, I threw up! No way was I having that stripe! I waited for the tailors to sew them on correctly and in good time. Andy still to this day doesn't get why I refused to accept it!

Chapter 5

Getting to and from Germany

The exercise season in Germany in the countryside was for about two months, September and October saw the full-scale divisional exercises. Our battalion deployed around this period although we did participate in similar exercises throughout the year, but only as a small headquarters group.

Exercises in the open country were an eye opener, you just used the land as you would see fit, it would not be unusual to see tanks ploughing through a field of potatoes, or combat engineers digging up someone's lawn for a defensive position.

We just use to roll into a farm yard and take over as if we owned it. Quite bizarre really, a left over from the end of WW2 when Germany was a defeated nation. As the unit exercising this had its advantages, after several days living compo rations the opportunity to inhabit a barn would always bring the best out in our chefs.

Negotiations with farmers usually produced little bonuses, we could use their bathrooms and get cleaned up and do a bit of laundry. Eggs and vegetables were obtained and in exchange we used to fill up the farmers cars and farm implements with petrol and diesel.

The fuel was issued on 'best guess' disguised as exercise accounting. So many deals were done using a bit of excess fuel. Times were changing though, by the 1980s and Germany was a significant voice at the table of European politics.

This sort of behaviour was becoming unacceptable to all parties. Firstly, the local population were unhappy at the destruction of land and property, they were becoming more affluent and attitudes of the younger generation were very different to post war generation. Secondly all exercises cost money.

A group of officers would follow the exercise and after the units had moved on, would negotiate compensation from landowners amounting in some cases to several thousand Deutschmarks! All units had to provide 'Damage Control' DAMCON as it was known but this consisted of half a dozen disinterested private soldiers, and an NCO armed with spades and brooms, quite ineffective really.

One of the rumours abounded after Exercise Lionheart was that cheques were written to the tunes of 10m DM! I can believe this based on what I witnessed in our area of operations.

Most deployments would be straightforward; we would catch a ferry late on a Friday night, and drive to our allotted area in the Sibbesse gap south west of the town of Hildesheim. Our advance party of company guides and the Quartermaster's department, would be in place to place us into our allotted areas. The battalion vehicles would form up either in Canterbury of the barracks at Dover, prior to moving to the docks.

On the road move to Germany in 1982 we were to move to Dunkirk in a commercial ferry that just transported lorries, these were much smaller than the normal ferries and prone to be thrown about severely in bad weather.

This particular year the winter storms had come early, we had had well over a month's rain in four days with gale force winds coming along the English Channel in tremendous gusts. Not exactly the weather to cross the channel.

The channel tunnel was still on the drawing board so it was either sit in the docks for two weeks or be a little brave. Even boarding the vessel was a drama; we had to wait until the ship came up from the swell before making a rush up the ramp before the vessel dropped away again. Not a good start to a night drive to Germany.

One year, 1983 I recall, we had all loaded and secured in the hold, we assembled in the restaurant on board to be told we had all the food we could eat, oh and by the way we were now going to Ostend instead due to the port at Dunkirk closed. A ferry had hit the loading ramp which couldn't be repaired until the weather improved.

We were told the infrastructure was not there to greet us; The Royal Corps of Transport Movements team didn't have an office at Ostend and would not travel up from Dunkirk to meet us because they were likely to get wet!

Myself and Pete Bartlett, the sergeant from the REME were briefed we would have to marshal the convoy on arrival, which meant the random way the ferry had been loaded had to be unravelled on the docks to ensure a competent commander was in the lead vehicle in the group and briefed on the new route.

The drivers were all ill from the throwing around of the ferry and the food in the hotplates was hardly touched other than by a few diehards. I have a stomach in line with a horse so the world was my oyster.

The chefs on board had cooked a marvellous stew with sprouts and mashed swede, undoubtedly this was one of my favourite meals but only three of us partook of this delicious feast. The chefs were tasked to provide packed meals so having plenty of time and a surplus of food; these were of a high standard.

On the docks at Ostend a most inhospitable environment awaited the REME sergeant and myself. Pete was an ex regular REME fitter/recovery mechanic who had joined up in the early 1950s and had been posted to Egypt initially but was then posted to a small unit based in Libya.

His task was to search the desert for abandoned vehicles from WW2 and recover them to base. This seemed a mundane job but it was quite an important task.

During the desert battles of 1941/42 many Axis soldiers were killed in the desert and during the course of the recovery, many bodies were discovered. With the extreme heat they had mummified in the positions where they had fallen.

Pete had done this for many years and had received a special medal from the Italian government for the recovery of their countryman's remains. After he was demobilised Pete had then gone on to be a London bus driver then joined the TA a few years later. Pete was a font of knowledge and a much-respected individual. Sadly, at the time of writing, he is no longer with us.

The wind and rain were blowing horizontally across the concrete basin. The last stop had been somewhere in the middle of the Atlantic Ocean.

Our showerproof waterproofs were soddened in seconds, together with all our uniform we wore. After two hours we had organised the convoys, ensured the fuel stops could be reached on what we held in the fuel tanks.

After the vehicles pulled away out of sight we climbed into the cab of our truck and assessed the situation. The truck was an old Bedford 3 ton RL nearly ready to be consigned to the scrap yard. The engine was petrol driven and accessible via a lift up cover in the cab.

This engine became very hot and the heat permeated up into the cab. In practise this was the only heat in the cab, great in winter but sweltering and stifling in the summer. We had our overalls in the cab so we decided to strip off and wear our overalls, beret and newly issued 'green' trainers for the journey into Germany.

We took it in turns to put the sodden clothes on the engine cover to dry. By the time we met up with the back end of the convoy at the border crossing at Venlo, they had almost dried. On arrival at the battalion assembly area, we dressed and got on with our normal duties.

For the next couple of days Pete complained he had a stomach ache. In the end we bullied him into visit the doctor. It transpired that Pete's thirty eight inch waist had my thirty four inch waist trousers round it! I hadn't noticed as I wore braces and hadn't noticed how baggy the ones I was wearing were!

On the major exercises such as Lionheart or Eternal triangle the road move would be more convoluted. Many units would be deploying from the UK over several days, the whole move would be orchestrated by the RMP, staging and refuelling areas would be located in woods within easy access of the autobahn. These were fine, but too much time was spent waiting for a slot to re-join the route.

These convoys could stretch back for miles, in particular, when armour and engineer equipment was moving. These vehicles could only move at around fifteen miles per hour, and the faster vehicles were held back until an appropriate gap.

Feeding arrangements for the road party were quite farcical. The army has always believed that the soldiers need to be fed well during moves. That principle is fine for the main body of soldiers travelling by air from Brize Norton, issued with the standard issue cardboard box with an apple and sausage roll freshly run over by a steamroller, but for the road party the boat was certainly pushed out.

During the time on the road the lunch box given to us on the boat plus one further meal would have been very adequate, but during each fuel and rest stop we would receive a hot meal.

The composite field ration comprised of, and indeed still does, a ten-man pack, a four-man pack and a twenty-four-hour individual pack. The ten- and four-man packs were primarily tinned food with dry packets and the twenty-four-hour pack evolved into boil in the bag food which was very tasty and nutritious.

In these rest stops division would arrange for a portion of units in Germany to provide chefs, mechanics and support staff to deal with the many units moving through a pre-determined location. Inevitably this was usually in a wooded area. The base chefs were issued each unlimited ten-man packs and to keep things simple. The main meal was a tinned meat option, a tin of mixed watery vegetables and instant potato. The tinned desert was usually sliced cake/pudding which had last seen the cold light of day thirty years before!

Because they did not know exact timings of arrival, no mobile phones in those days! These were kept warm in the field cookers. Although the tinned steak was palatable it was not easy to portion so the chefs preferred the 15oz tin of steak and kidney pudding.

One tin of the pudding would feed two people; it was cut in half cold and warmed up on a tray. It used to collapse and the pudding went white. The more discerning of the lads described them as 'baby's heads', quite why leaves a lot to the imagination!

We were staged far too many times, given two jerry cans of petrol at each stop and the obligatory meal of baby's heads. I still can't comprehend just how accounting differed on a major exercise. Back in barracks every drop of fuel, oil, wiper blades and bulb had to be accounted for in a system of double accounting, on exercise it was a different matter. Our vehicles were usually full to the brim and storing ten plus jerry cans of fuel became problematical.

On leaving the staging area, you would see piles of jerry cans dumped as the drivers had no means of storing them.

When you are driving in convoy you move at a set speed for miles without change. All you see is the rear light of the vehicle in front with the snake of slow-moving vehicles disappearing into the distance on the long lazy bends of the autobahn. You need to remain alert and not full of stodge! No matter how much rest you had in the days prior to the road move you were always tired and exhausted.

On Exercise Lionheart in 1984, my record for baby's heads was seven in eighteen hours together with twenty-four cans of fuel. Sleep was not an option, way before the EU regulations and driver's hours and working time regulations etc. There were accidents and injuries over the years but nothing too serious.

When we arrived at a pre-determined point, usually near the rear echelon of the brigade we would be met by guides and then led in complete darkness to our respective area. This was always the most fraught part of the road move.

We had maps that showed us to the rear area, but when the air party arrived, they moved into positions within the battalion area which we didn't have sight of.

This meant that small groups were moving on tracks and small roads just focussing on a five-watt bulb shining on a small white disc on the axle of the vehicle in front. Sounds simple but in reality, the disc was filthy from 400 miles of road dirt, extreme tiredness played a part together with numbness and sore eyes, really didn't help.

This always seemed to be at three am with icy rain falling like stair rods. The plains of Germany had a prevailing wind which had a last stop in Siberia.

What was truly remarkable, after we camouflaged the vehicles with nets and hessian, 3 hours sleep provided enough to recharge the batteries, after that we used to run on adrenaline.

There was always the deadline to get back to the ferry. They were mostly civilian ferries operating their normal schedules. After 2 weeks living rough in the field, working 20-hour days, we would be moved to a barracks for a shower and hot food. A good night rest and off just after breakfast.

Derek Mirams was the Mechanical Transport officer was very much old school, a former company Sergeant Major in the Buffs TA, you were not allowed to overtake him on route and woe betide if you did.

At the next rest stop you learned the ways of perfect spacing, fuel economy and the fact you had to guard the vehicles whilst everyone had a meal! He would always be watching. One of his infuriating foibles was to get all the vehicles lined up perfectly when you look down the row! This took hours every day and wasted so much fuel shuffling vehicles for his fetish and inevitably dinner was cold by the time you arrived!

All that said he was knowledgeable and underneath all the red-faced shouting, he had a heart of gold, and only wanted the best for his guys.

On return to home barracks, you had to check and clean the weapons, account for all the stores, declare 'exercise losses' so they could be written off against the exercise costs and eventually replaced.

Radio batteries and rifle magazines were always claimed. One year we lost a trailer at a rest stop we thought another unit passing through the rest stop were short of one and ours looked appealing it was unhitched and long gone before anyone noticed!

Even after all these years I still don't know the final outcome of the enquiry. The trailer was a small ¾ tonne version towed by a land rover. The amount of kit contained within was amazing; I deduced that the contents of this particular trailer weighed thirteen and a half tonnes, quite remarkable!

All the lost stores over the last ten years suddenly were replaced. This sometimes backfired when a civilian handed in a rifle to the police in Wales, having found it leaning up against his car on a ferry bound for Dover!

A few days after the return from exercise whilst back at work, I had to do a vehicle recovery on the A2 just outside of Dover; this guy had a very old and seriously worn-out camper van, which had finally breathed its last after a summer going around Europe. I had just finished winching the vehicle up and lashing down the wheels when I saw something familiar in the bushes.

On inspection it was ten jerry cans of Lionheart petrol, I guess another unit had gone by this lay-by and had a clear out of surplus items, looking more closely I found six ten-man ration packs, a rifle magazine and sling!

I collected everything up and later in the day popped round to the barracks and handed in most of the stash! Four jerry cans of petrol kept my Honda 90 going for over a year. The down side of this I bitterly regret now was the army petrol. This was the equivalent of the old two star my Honda should have run on four stars! The cylinder head exploded and cost me more than the equivalent of the four cans of fuel!

Chapter 6

Learning the craft

As an MT driver you are called upon to undertake all sorts of tasks, whether it was to drive the ambulance with the Doctor and medics to Sennybridge training area to provide medical emergency cover, or drive recruits to Catterick.

All of this was on a Friday night after a long and tiring week at work. Our Battalion was chosen as the centre of excellence for officer training by our masters at that time, South East District who were based in Aldershot.

We were to provide the basic training for officer cadets from right across the region. We handpicked the best instructors from the adjacent units and trained jointly for one weekend per month.

This training produced some of the very best officers I have ever known, many of that group went onto very senior roles and I am still in contact with several of that era. Most of the top students at Sandhurst were from this group.

One particular weekend the allocated driver was on holiday abroad so I was tasked as the driver for the weekend. Initially I thought this would be a good job after a horrendous week at work. How wrong was I!

When I arrived to pick up the minibus, I was advised it had not returned from its previous duty. I was given a very unusual vehicle I had never driven before. It was a land rover 110, a one tonne load carrying vehicle, which were normally used by the Mortar platoon in Guildford but this one had been with us for a while for driver training.

This vehicle was forward control, that is to say the driver sat above the wheels so the steering was more reactive. They were very nippy because the engine was the Rover 3.5 litre containing many more horses than the usual land rover engine.

The one thing about this vehicle was it had an extremely high centre of gravity. Because of the need to move cross country the wheel clearance meant the body was unusually high. They were prone to tipping over when going over rough ground even at slow speed, and more dangerously by cornering very fast.

Some very nasty accidents occurred over the years with these vehicles but luckily none of them were in our unit. In later years this vehicle was pensioned off and replaced by a Steyer Puch Pinzegauer which was a much better vehicle with a lower centre of gravity.

I loaded the kit, was given a map to Crowborough training area. I had heard that this area was in the Ashdown Forest home of Winnie the Pooh so I looked forward to seeing what it was like. The training area was a couple of miles away from the training camp which itself was overlooking forests and rolling heath land.

I had been told by my grandfather many years earlier that when he had joined the TA in the early 1930s, he had marched from Folkestone to Crowborough camp for their annual training period. four days to get there and four back with two days actual training in between!

The training area was on long lease from the local landowner. It was several thousand acres of woodland, heath and fields set in the stunning backdrop of the Ashdown Forest with a herd of red deer roaming freely.

On arrival, I was advised that I would be helping the training team for the weekend. The officer cadets went patrolling and practising tactics during the day, and then retired to a hillside to dig in for the night.

This proved to be a very soggy and wet experience for the trainee Rupert's as the water running downwards from where we sat at the top of hill, filled the trenches with water. The soil on the training area was sandy and therefore easy to construct a reasonable defensive hole in less than an hour.

The training team made a waterproof basha area to the rear of this slope so not to interfere with the training. One of the training team was a real character; he worked for the MOD and had access to kit and equipment we could only dream of. He had arranged a loan of a couple of Humber Pigs to transport the enemy about and to attack the defensive position.

During the late afternoon it began to rain heavily and the air hung damp in the hollow in front of the hillside. I was tasked with the safety radio (I didn't even know how to switch it on!) and the two inch mortar. This was a simple weapon capable of launching a high explosive round three hundred meters. We had illuminating rounds on parachute flares for this exercise which I began to dismantle from its packaging.

I worked out that you put the mortar into the tube, place it firmly on the ground and when you are ready point the tube towards the enemy and pull the cord!

I constructed a shelter to keep dry and sat waiting for instructions. I noted that we had about eighty of these mortar bombs and reflecting back this was the most I ever saw in my whole career in one place. The date on the box was 1951 so clearly the ordnance depot was having a clear out!

I was given about thirty thunder flashes and shown how to prepare them, again I had never thrown one. The instructor then explained that I was to provide the simulated grenade noise and to do this I had to do something completely illegal.

Thunder flashes should never be filled with soil because this could be extremely dangerous to eyes and other exposed body parts if they went off too close to someone. To get the range down the hill they were too light, the simplest way of adding weight was to stuff them with sand-the big no no.

I was advised to throw them to my left where there was nobody too close. I duly stripped them down to expose the igniters' and filled their tube with the soft sand from the hillside.

One of the battalion armourers arrived with a general-purpose machine gun. He explained that the cocking handle had been snapped off; he continued to say that when you initially cock the weapon, you have to push the handle completely forward before firing it otherwise the handle flew apart. The training team needed the machine gun to give the effect of a more sustained attack to added realism to the officer cadets dug in below me.

I had a look at the gun and it seemed to me you could cock the weapon using a combination tool from a rifle cleaning kit, and if it was balanced properly wouldn't need to be cocked again unless you ran out of ammunition.

I was given 24,000 rounds of blank ammunition and told to fire in long bursts when instructed. So, there I was on top of a hill, sitting crossed legged with a machine gun to my left and open boxes of ammunition, a mortar to my right with stacks of rounds ready to go. Under my poncho were the thunder flashes keeping dry.

The shout 'Gun' came up the hill so I fired the gun in bursts of ten rounds and then the shout 'light' so I popped off a couple of illuminating rounds. The command 'grenade' was shouted and I struck an igniter and threw the thunder flash as hard as I could!

The attack came in, the pigs were charging about dropping off more guys, the noise was tremendous. The words Gun, Light and Grenade kept coming and I kept firing. After what seemed like hours the last flickering parachute flare died away with the fading light, the scene below in the valley was shrouded in smoke and the rain still came down. Silence prevailed across the valley.

The smell of cordite filled the air and a strange uneasy feeling prevailed. The area in front of me seemed very dark; the only sounds audible were the distant sound of a tawny owl. The officer in charge, Major John Fowler, came up and congratulated me on getting the gun going and putting up light when needed but he started to laugh at the scene.

I was sitting in a heap of blank cartridges, the gun barrel was steaming and clicking and piles of empty ammo boxes strewn around. He said it looked like I had just finished a battle at Khe San at the height of the Vietnam war. An uneventful night followed and in the morning the officer cadets were given the task of cleaning the machine gun. This was a laborious task and usually undertaken by several people. I just watched and smiled, poor officer cadets!

Chapter 7

Aspirations

It was clear from the start the best job as a driver was the guy who drove the Mechanical Transport Officer. He helped to put up the command post and added and maintained the camouflage nets etc. The lucky guy who did this was excused from digging trenches and guard duty.

He was the MTO's PA, did his errands, cooked his food and generally had it easy. Having seen him looking very smug in clean dry clothes, shaven and well rested, I vowed I would get that job.

The following year my campaigning worked and I was promoted to corporal and sent on a course to learn how the radios worked, more about this course later. My predecessor was promoted to MT Sergeant and now did his stint driving for hours and being wet and cold with not more than a little resentment it must be said!

My plan did backfire slightly, because I now knew how to work the radios, I was called upon to change frequencies and change antennas when communications were lost. Far less sleep than I ever imagined I would get.

I always had the watch at midnight to change the frequencies and change batteries etc. The radios we had at this time were the Larkspur range. They were pre digital and difficult to tune. They dated from the 1950s and you had to be a good operator to make them work, these sets needed skill!

When the Clansman range of radios were issued, it took away some of the expertise and intuition needed. They were digital with a built-in squelch and set length antenna. This meant more sleep for me!

One late afternoon on an exercise in Germany, the MTO asked if I could run some telephone line into the Railway station in Else. This was a railhead where several rail lines met. We were parked up in the railway yard. There was not much going on so I complied with the request.

I relayed the radio via the line into the station and flicked the switch. A little later the watch keeper rota was changed to reflect the fact our commander and a couple of the sergeants were 'out of the Echelon' I thought no more and had a ten-hour sleep!

When I awoke all of the key personalities had changed, that's what you get for having a few beers when you are on a dry exercise! Unbeknown to me they were in the station bar and had to subsequently sleep off the effects of the beer they had consumed.

We all felt a bit jealous but drinking on exercise was 'verboten' and we all knew the penalties. The German police had loaded guns and there was a zero policy on drink driving.

Over the years I maintained my skills with the Signals platoon and progressed to the next qualification level. Towards the end of my career, I became acting Regimental Signals Officer as part of my duties as OC HQ company as the post was vacant.

Having been in the Echelon for a while as the MTO's driver I coveted another job I considered I could do well without too much sleep loss.

The mechanics of the Royal Electrical and Mechanical Engineers detachment needed spare parts. The unit carried a 4-ton truck with a large trailer containing the replacement tyres and exhausts etc. There was a great deal of spare time involved in this job. The person in charge was the technical sergeant who was stores/accounts trained and a private soldier who was a driver.

The truck was stacked with loose cardboard boxes but this would involve considerable rummaging and cussing. The inevitable nature of the work the REME needed the smallest and most buried part at 2am!

I was promoted to sergeant and was given the stores job. I made some changes to the way we worked the spare parts issue. I had seen some large green fibre glass bins in the back of a truck when scrounging from an adjacent unit. They had removable fronts which joined together.

I managed to get the part number of one from one of these boxes. They were known as Thomas bins, used throughout BAOR. In the army you can't ask for anything unless you know the part number! I was able to order spare parts relevant to vehicle breakdowns and routine maintenance.

I decided to try and see if I could confuse the system and order one of these bins. I could not believe it when a bin arrived about a month later. I ordered a further thirty-nine and then proceeded to mount them in the back of the stores truck. One row down each side, and a double row in the centre.

I was praised for my ingenuity and how it would improve efficiency. From the outside it looked great, just right for the task. What they didn't see was the bunk beds in the depths of the truck for me and the driver! At last, a bit of comfort.

Over the years the cost of running an army went sky high, spare parts availability was reduced and stock levels you were allowed to hold was cut by 75%. This freed up bin space in the truck so Bennett enterprises set up a shop selling chocolate bars commonly known as claccy, cans of coke and it was not unknown for a few crates of beer to be 'in stock' After all I was the son of a grocer!

When we were in the UK there were lines of vehicles unusable waiting for a crucial part. As we crept towards our deployment to BAOR the priority for spares was increased so we could repair all the vehicles to deploy. Because the stocks were minimal it meant ordering spares through the exercise system. We had to wait for them longer than we were available in theatre.

This meant leaving vehicles behind and collecting them some months later. To avoid this scenario the stores sergeant went to the brigade and scrounged parts from the units permanently based in Germany. This involved being away from base for many hours at a time, having driven hundreds of kilometres.

This activity was usually done in a land rover or on Harley Davison trials bike that we were supplied with. This meant the driver could still operate the 'shop' whilst I was away.

Feeding was always a problem during this time. The chefs didn't save you meals and you didn't have time to produce compo. The locals were intuitive; they always had a portable van which sold German sausage and chips surreptitiously parked closed to deployed army units.

The Schnell Imbiss produced the mainstay of Bratwurst mitt Frites unt mayonnaise of Currywurst with Kartoffelen etc. Day or night you could always get a cheap meal with strong coffee for a couple of Deutschmarks. How they made a living heaven knows!

When you were in a tactical position for more than a couple of days you would be cheered up if you heard a grumbling engine and the occasional horn sound more like a throttled duck – it would be Wolfgang or someone with a similar name, and his mobile bratty van, through years following the troops exercising he made a good living selling bratties coke and claccy knowing exactly where they would be!

There must have been hundreds of Wolfgang's all across West Germany! I can't imagine Wolfgang setting up shop the other side of the Inner German border somehow, the conscripts in the East were very poorly paid in comparison.

I suppose I was very naive when I joined up and started to progress through the system. Working through the echelon system you were not really exposed to the level of tactical awareness that the guys dug in the front line were.

The daily briefing consisted of technical information such as ammunition resupply, feeding timings for the forward positions and general resupply issues. When we went out of the echelon we had to book in and out so the commander knew where we were.

In passing you would ask where the enemy front line was so you could mark it on the map. If you strayed into an enemy position, you were captured and made to dig trenches when the umpires were not looking! Everyone knew where the enemy was!

During my time out and about in the West German countryside I noted just how beautiful it was, from mountainous regions in the South and East to the long rolling uplands and plains very much reminiscent of Salisbury plain but with more trees.

Having time and of course needing rest breaks I noticed certain things that made the landscape different to ours; the electricity pylons all sat on concrete plinths where were approximately four feet high, it took me a while to work this out as it seems a little odd.

One of four supports was different to the others; the concrete plinth had dozens of small holes built in to it, initially I thought it might be something to do with securing a ladder for maintenance.

On road bridges just short of the drop to the valley there were strips across the road with preformed circular holes, there were also similar strips with the same holes in cuttings, about ten feet up from some road surfaces.

After chatting to a driver from the Royal Engineers at a schnell imbiss one day I learned why these unusual features were in place. During the reconstruction after WW2 the threat from the Soviet Union became more real.

The Soviets were posturing from the late 1940s and it became clear that they had aspirations to hold territory across mainland Europe. The holes were prebuilt into roads, and the rail and road bridge abutments.

If the day came and the attack was imminent the holes took explosive charges which would be detonated to cause a potential enemy to be delayed. Looking again at the pylons it was clear they were set to fall across roads etc.

They had an unusual nickname, they were known as measles holes, when challenged the driver said look at your exercise map. When this was scrutinised the roads and railway lines there were red dots where these measles holes existed. What a good idea I thought easy to find, but then the first map to fall into Soviet hands would have revealed all the key routes right across West Germany!

One day a new toy was delivered, it was a standard flatbed 4 ton truck with a modified fire retardant plate behind the cab. Mounted on the back were two 2200 litre fuel tanks that could be used to carry both petrol and diesel or linked to deliver one fuel, as time progressed petrol vehicles were phased out and diesel was used for every vehicle.

This was known by the acronym UBRE to the layman this was a Unit Bulk Refuelling Equipment. The potential for getting out and about independently and avoiding watch keeper duties was becoming more palatable. I had to learn how to work this beast.

This machine was certainly a step up, the labour involved in refuelling the battalion was indescribable. Carrying three days' worth of fuel in jerry cans used to eat into our stores and troop-carrying abilities. We never deployed with all our vehicles, there was always a couple left behind for one reason or another, and of course accidents and breakdowns took out a certain percentage.

We didn't hold enough jerry cans to undertake such an adventure. We had to order them and collect them from West Moors in Somerset. As always, the collection date was fixed by the army so on the day of the royal wedding of Charles and Diana, my friend Pete Bartlett and I were on the road in a truck collecting fuel cans.

When crossing to the continent all these cans had to be washed out with a steam cleaner and vented, this applied to the UBRE, we used to take it to a fuel terminal at Coryton in Essex to get the equipment flushed through.

Once we had crossed the channel both the UBRE and the fuel can truck used to go off separately to one of the major refuelling depots to top up the cans and the tanks on the vehicle.

The drivers of these vehicles usually arrived just as we deployed on exercise having had no time to change their clothes or shower. When we went home the two fuel vehicles would be driven by the permanent staff. We usually returned back to the UK on a Saturday morning after the post exercise wash up and kit check late on a Friday.

The rules on the continent and the civilian staff at these huge locations only worked weekdays. The guys used to have to park up and wait until Monday morning before they could unload the residual fuel and get the tanks flushed. They arrived back in Canterbury on Tuesday evening.

The army logistics system was very efficient and well tried and tested over many years. The rule of thumb for wheeled vehicles was you had three days' worth of fuel with you in the unit. One day equalled the ability to drive one hundred miles.

The first day's fuel was held in the tanks of the vehicles themselves; the second day was at the first line which was in cans at A1 echelon and the third day was either on board the UBRE or cans ground dumped at the A2 echelon with the stores and troop-carrying vehicles.

For all the front line companies resupply was undertaken at night, whether it was refuelling, rations water or ammunition. It was always believed the Soviets had a limited night vision capability so they should have been blind to the vehicle movements. Of course, nothing was further from the truth; it transpired they had an equal capability.

After the tanks were emptied on the resupply the remaining fuel was decanted into jerry cans or into vehicles at the echelon the UBRE made the tedious trip to the nearest fuel depot.

The brigade did have 22,000 litre tankers and ground tanks but these seemed to be exclusive for the armoured vehicles, so we had to travel 200km round trip and wait in a queue to top up tanks.

This was very tiring work and usually two drivers worked on a rota. I began to wish I had never seen one of these machines. After a couple of years more operators were trained and the task became less onerous.

Chapter 8

Signals training

I had always been fascinated with radio communication and it was in my blood. My uncle was a member of the RSGB before WW2 and went on to be a radar technician in the war. He joined the RAF and after his training he was posted to Folkestone.

At Capel le Ferne there is a large white house on the cliffs edge. This was a fledgling VHF listening station. They worked in tandem with the code breakers at Bletchley Park. They decoded the shorter-range VHF signals from the German units stationed near Calais. They obtained the details of unit moves, unit designations and more importantly as D day neared, whether units were moving towards Normandy to reinforce the defences, or participate in a counter attack.

My uncle worked there under strict secrecy. After the war he advised that the enemy knew about it and sent fighters to shoot it up the antennas nearly every day. He told me he was nearly hit quite a few times.

Quite bizarrely he came from the Capel end of Folkestone but was not allowed to visit home. His letters to his mum never let on he was stationed less than a mile from the family home.

My mother was in the RAF and retrained during this period to be a radio operator on Morse code radio sets. She did allude to working at the Dover castle tunnel complex but it may only have been for a very short period.

I attended Canterbury College for an evening course to gain the amateur radio qualification when I was fourteen. We learned to build basic radios that worked on the high frequency range and how to fault find etc.

One of the most useful things I learned how to make was used a few years later, it was a device called a lossy toroid. This was a circular piece of carbon wrapped with copper cable.

We had a powerful RAF radar station in the next village and when you were watching the television a fuzzy blip appeared on the screen every thirty seconds day and night! I simply connected both ends to TV aerial connectors and the problem vanished.

I made many of these for neighbours and desperate people in the village for five pounds each in 1984, was a good return for my minimal effort!

When the chance to use the military radios came, I jumped at the chance. As I had said before the interest was always there but I had joined to get an HGV licence so the mould was set. In 1980 I was sent to West Down camp on Salisbury Plain to attend a course with the Signals platoon.

We learned about the capabilities of the sets, voice procedure and how to send messages in code. This was interspersed with short practical exercises which were great fun.

It didn't rain for two weeks so that added to the enjoyment. Our instructors were very knowledgeable and easy going so the course was over before I knew it.

The radios we used were in the Larkspur range, they dated back to the late 1950s, and they were all knocked about and a little thin on paint in places. The radios you could carry were heavy but the weight was mainly the batteries which were almost as big as the sets and you had to carry a spare as well.

The section radio was the A40, this had a range of about two kilometres and a choice of antenna systems, the platoon radio was the A41, this was a little larger but you needed to be quite skilled to operate this set, you had to tune it by selecting the frequency, then gently operating the tuning knob and lock it at the precise point of optimum sound. The general rule of thumb was never to fiddle with it once locked!

Another man pack radio which could be clipped in the back of a land rover was the A13. This set together with all the others in the range was analogue, but this one was the long-range set that required a combination of skills of siting antennas and again a tuning swing for the best connection. you had to tune it by swinging a needle and lock it at the precise point of optimum sound.

To ensure everyone was on the same frequency the base station would give out a netting call. Each radio net was identified by two letters, i.e., B and E, the control station would transmit for one minute after frequency change the two letters phonetically continuously without letting go of the prestle switch for example, 'BE' 'BE' 'BE' etc. In this time, you had to change the frequency and swing the needle when the voice on the other end was loudest and flick the lock switch.
The HF frequency was thought to be unable to be tracked by direction finding hence the long uninterrupted transmission.

This radio was used for the resupply net as the distances could be up to thirty-five kilometres. When our VHF sets were being jammed, we reverted to the A13 as it wasn't affected by jamming signals.

We always had this set turned on, it was tuned into 6090 MHz which was the BBC world service where the news and an accurate time signal could be obtained. Over the years the HF set became a huge part of my world, whether as an operator or a watchkeeper and commander. The sound of a distant station fading in and out on the carrier wave became strangely comforting.

I worked with the signals platoon more frequently, I was released by the MT when there was Signals training going on outside of battalion exercises, I would attend training with them to increase my skills.

In 1981 when we were with 6 Field force, they put a great deal on emphasis on telephone line laying. They held an annual competition in Aldershot just before the summer leave period.

The TA units were not normally involved in this as the competition was held in the week. Regular army formations generally don't work weekends unless it's a formal exercise or a deployment, so outside of these times we were not used to seeing the guys around.

Field telephones were used frequently in BAOR as a counter measure the EMP (electromagnetic pulse) that is given out by a nuclear explosion. This would take out our radios, so telephones were the only way to communicate with our sub units.

I used to be amazed when two guys would appear at the echelon with a telephone twelve kilometres behind the battalion command post! Suddenly the radio operator became a telephone operator and a much easier life ensued for him.

When the competition was notified to us, we held two training weekends to do with everything line laying. From burying it, to crossing obstacles, wet and dry, railway lines, all the drills to finding breaks and faults. We knew line inside out. I loved the brackets you strapped to your ankles to shin up trees!

When we arrived at Aldershot (pre M25 so it took about four hours to drive from Canterbury) it was clear the competition was fierce, looking at the scores of the regulars who had done the course over the previous few days, we had a lot to do. The opposition all arrived, ranging from the Intelligence corps to the engineers, signals squadrons and the guys from 10 Para.

Looking at the opposition it was clear no one was going to set the world alight, no one had done specific training for the competition except us so we didn't admit anything. What stood out to us was the shine on the Para's. They were spotless, shiny boots and not a thing out of place, what was most striking about them was they ran as a group everywhere. We sauntered and wandered about like the scruffy guys we were, we didn't care.

Attending the weekend was a bit touch and go for me, I had been suffering with hay fever in the previous week and the slight cough I had, was moving to my chest. Not to let anyone down, I turned up and was excused the driving so I could get some rest.

We had to attend a briefing and found out we had to have three rolls of line, we smiled as we had been using five for the training! A start time was set for each team and we sat and waited our turn.

Part of the skill for line laying is navigation on the ground, you had to know how to use a map and compass very well. The allotted time came for us to make our way to the start line, each team has a 30-minute interval between the next group so we waited for the Para's to go.

They didn't have the line carriers we had to safely secure the rolls, they simply held them above their heads and started to run. We couldn't contain ourselves; they went in a completely wrong direction!

Our turn came and we set off, checking in every few minutes with base and advising of our progress, after fifteen minutes we came to a junction in the woods and across our front ran the para's. Still trailing the line and again the rolls above their heads and still going the wrong way!

We continued to a mock-up of a railway line which we negotiated quite well and just as we approached the finish line the Para's once again crossed our front and disappeared out of site oblivious to the end of the course.

They suddenly reappeared and considerably red and puffing, crossed the finish a few yards ahead of us. Being Queen's men, the whole idea of the game was to produce a technically correct line lay. Yes, speed was important but the technical element was the main event.

When the scores were done and the 'Royal Signals' experts had adjudicated, the Para's were deemed winners! Jim was red with rage and complained loudly anyone who would listen that 'these paras can't be up to much if they were beaten (Jim never accepted that we didn't win) by a midget (him) a Michelin man (Nick) and a cripple (me, I was covered in blood from nose bleeds)

The Para's line was all slack and obvious to see, not tactical at all! It makes you wonder sometimes if these things are influenced. The General was wearing a red beret, fancy that? The only saving grace was on Monday morning he called all his commanding officers in and ripped them a new backside each for allowing a bunch of butcher's bakers and candlestick makers beat all the regular teams. Overall, we came second behind the Para's so quite an achievement.

All this said, I was carried mostly by the other two guys in the team, Jim who I mentioned in the first chapter and Nick now a retired college lecturer, realised I was sinking. I felt awful, I had coughed and sneezed so much I had a nose bleed, and my eyes were so bloodshot and swollen from the hay fever, I couldn't see much at all.

After crossing the finish line and went to see the medics who initially thought I had suffered an accident. After a couple of paracetamols and antihistamine jab, I was told to have a rest.

When I went to the doctors on the Monday, I was told I was a complete idiot for going on the weekend and promptly sent me to hospital in an ambulance where I spent the next two weeks with severe pneumonia!

This episode didn't diminish my enthusiasm for all things army; I was better ready in time to go to the next big exercise in Denmark...

Chapter 9

Soldiers of the Queen...

Exercise Amber Express took the whole battalion to Denmark for the first time. This gave us the opportunity to forge the existing links with the Danes. HM Queen Margarethe of Denmark had been our honorary colonel in chief since 1967.

The whole of 6 Field Force had deployed a couple of weeks earlier so the road move there was only the TA units deploying. The 3rd Battalion of our regiment had joined the brigade recently, following their recent handover from the Royal Hampshire regiment in the barracks in Dover. This was the first time we had exercised with them as complete units.

The journey to Harwich was uneventful, having re fuelled in Colchester at the home of our 2nd Battalion we arrived at the port to find the place had virtually closed down due to inclement weather, when I say inclement it was gale force winds, driving waves and freezing spray.

This was to be a rerun of the trip of 1978, we looked forward to sixteen hours across the North Sea to Esbjerg. With the wind direction and the sea swell, this was in reality twenty-two hours. We felt awful and didn't look forward to the next part of the journey.

The exercise was south of Copenhagen so it meant catching another ferry to Zealand. We were not happy warriors at the thought of this; in particular the ferry was booked containing the road party of 10 Para. There had always been animosity between the battalions, a friendly rivalry that had always existed between the two battalions both believing they were better soldiers.

We all boarded the ferry but it didn't cast off. We sat in port with the ramp down for two hours. Eventually a car approached the ferry; it was an old-style Rolls Royce. Fascinated by such an unusual sight we all hung over the rear rail peering to see who this could be.

The car disappeared into the hold and we were off in just a few moments. The passenger of the car was none other than the Queen of Denmark, our Colonel in Chief! She came up to the restaurant and when she recognised the cap badge she was in her element, talking to the guys and having coffee with the officers.

This was the ultimate revenge on 10 Para, when the hierarchy realised our Colonel in Chief was here, they all sidled down below to the lorry driver's cafe and sulked!

We disembarked separately and we watched in complete amazement as their anti-tank platoon drove down the ramp in their stripped-down land rovers and onto the docks wearing not their red berets but horned Viking helmets! What a bunch of posers, nothing like upsetting the locals.

The area we were billeted in was on a hillside which was fine; the views were amazing until it started to rain, and rain it did for the rest of our stay. We had to dig gulley's around our tents to divert the water. This was a very uncomfortable stay, made worse by the latrines at the bottom of the field. This flooded out after a couple of days and life became more difficult.

After two days we deployed on exercise. We tended to stay in farms and not in open country so as I was the echelon commander's driver, the experience became quite pleasant based mainly indoors and not exposed to the elements. After the first move we stayed in the same farm for the duration.

We got on well with the farmer, he put down fresh straw in the unused pig pens but the animals were only a few feet away and the smell was unbelievable. We were all pleased when we had to wear our gasmasks and quite sad when they had to be put away!

The guard duties and watchkeeping for a change on this exercise were quite minimal, so we had some time on our hands. The weather was cold and generally damp, so inside was always a good option to while away the hours. During the chit chat and banter that always occurs in down time, someone asked where you could find the joints of meat on a real pig.

After some debate and leaning over the pen like some old yokel farmers, one of the guys appeared with a wide felt tipped marker pen. He said he had seen a diagram at work and said working it out was easy. Five minutes later he had used the marker pen on the nearest pig, stood back and admired his work of art! A white pig now covered in lines representing the meat joints, looked quite the picture, we dispersed and thought no more of it.

This is where Danish and British relations took a turn for the worse. A few hours later I awoke to a great deal of shouting! The farmer who up till now had been very friendly and helpful, was in the barn shouting at the top of his voice in Danish, pointing and yelling in a most furious manner; It would appear the pig, now portioned up nicely, was his show pig about to go to a local show the next day.

As hard as we might the black marker pen would not come off the pig's skin, the more we tried the crosser the pig became and the farmer became redder. The officer in charge of the echelon was incensed and wanted retribution, Captain Derek Mirams at his best!

No one knew anything nor was awake to testify. We all then were tactically despatched around the farm to dig trenches and erect overhead cover. Guard duties, up to this point had been a single individual at any one time became three! The company sergeant major was having a field day.

A driver was dispatched back to the quartermaster at B Echelon to collect twelve bottles of scotch and twenty jerry cans of diesel for farm machinery around the place. I also believe the guys back at base had a vegetarian stew that evening for supper; the farmer had more beef for his freezer than he could store.

I understand he contacted the organisers of his local show and told them the pig had died, they felt sorry for him and had a whip round to buy a new one!

When we left the farmer was most happy, the whole family came out to wave us goodbye with huge smiles on our faces. When we returned to camp there was an enquiry as to what happened.

Someone piped up they thought the culprit was a visitor from another unit on the exercise; this happened often and as no one knew a name the matter was dropped. There was muttering from the group in earshot of the commander that they thought the culprits had red berets sticking out of their jacket pockets!

During this period, we had a quartermaster who was a legend throughout the regiment. His name was Major Les Wilson MBE. He was a good QM and he always did his best for his unit.

Towards the end of his career, he was promoted to Lt Colonel which was unheard of in a unit. Lt Col QMs usually only were found at force level. I mention Les at this time because he was involved in another of my near misses. That year when he was the QM, we hosted an event at the Kent Show at Detling.

This involved moving the Officers mess silver, crockery and cutlery, together with most of the regimental silver, drums and all the usual things we used to supply to Detling. The two mess stewards, Howard Aldous and Dave Harris didn't hold an

HGV licence so I was asked to drive the truck to Detling on the Thursday morning and go back Sunday afternoon to collect it.

This worked well, I drove the vehicle up and returned in the land rover Dave had used. The event went well and I went back at 5pm on the Sunday as arranged. I met with Dave and Howard, they gave me the keys of the truck and hopped into the land rover and said see you back at base, in a flash they were gone!

I walked around the truck and thought it was sitting rather oddly, the Bedford RL was a 3-ton truck used to move either twenty people or light stores. This one was so laden the rear springs were reversed and it sat at a funny angle. I looked in the rear and to my surprise the mainly empty vehicle that I delivered before the weekend was loaded over the sides and the canvas had been tightened to hold things in.

There were white fences, turf, plants in concrete pots. flower troughs, flag poles, hedges in pots and sand bags full of sand in profusion. In the pre mobile phone days, I couldn't call anyone so had no choice but to drive this dangerous and overloaded truck gingerly home.

In those days the police tended to ignore army vehicles unless they were broken down so off, I went. I managed to get the vehicle into top gear going down Detling hill towards Sittingbourne but it began to run away, the brakes began to smell of burning and eventually I just managed to get it under control before I joined the motorway.

I chugged up the hills in second gear with the engine overheating and downhill with the brakes smelling and ineffective. The usual ¾ hour journey took two hours and when I returned to Leros, Dave and Howard had gone home fed up with waiting.

I reversed the truck up against the wall of the officer's mess tightly and put away the keys. I called the MT sergeant the next morning to complain and explain why I was so long returning. It appears the QM was approached by organisers and event crews to see if they wanted this stuff they were going to dump. He said yes at it would look good at the forthcoming cocktail party.

The following drill night I was informed the truck needed two new rear leaf springs, a clutch and complete new brake including drums, in fact it was almost a write off due to cost.

1981 saw the end of 6 Field Force. The formation ceased to exist on the 31st December with a different structure of operations in the regular army going forward. 6 Field Force morphed into an airmobile brigade consisting of the Parachute regiments.

We were assigned to 2 Infantry Brigade based at Shorncliffe, together with the infantry unit in Dover and at Howe barracks in Canterbury. This was the first time a regional administrative brigade had all its units within easy reach.

This change for us brought a different tempo of training, gone were the helicopters and Hercules, our unit scales on vehicles, radios and to some degree manpower gradually eroded over the next couple of years.

It wasn't until 1983 that the downward spiral was halted, we then were assigned to 33 Armoured Brigade as a reinforcement battalion and our expeditions to the plains of Germany started again in earnest.

This time it was different, we were still administered by 2 Brigade but we were very much involved in all matters BAOR, Our CO would fly out to attend orders groups and individuals used to deploy to fill slots make vacant by soldiers and officers who were on career courses. They also used to practise the battle casualty process frequently where you would make up the numbers after simulated casualties had been taken out of the exercise.

1982 saw the battalion at annual camp at Wretham in Norfolk. This camp was split into two halves, the first week was field firing and the second was an exercise. The middle weekend was split between a day off on Saturday and a slow start on Sunday then deploying late afternoon onto the training area.

The Officers and Sergeants messes had regimental dinners on the Saturday evening. During the first week I was ferrying soldiers to the ranges and doing general MT work, from changing tyres to picking up people from the station.

We had a driver from D Coy called Stone. He had been around a few years but I had never seen him before, I didn't really take to him as he was always moaning and complaining. If I had been the MT sergeant, I would have been very fed up with him as the mood amongst the guys was a bit low.

No one wanted to do duties with this guy and thought him a little odd. I allude to this because on the Saturday he was involved in a strange incident. I was the Duty driver based in the guard room for a twenty-four-hour duty missing the day off. I didn't really mind as I didn't fancy going to Norwich for the day.

I did a few jobs throughout the day and was reading a book when Stone booked out the guardroom to go to the local village and thought nothing of it. About nine pm, he came back into camp and booked in.

He was very aggressive and really quite nasty. The guard commander told him to go to bed so off he went. About thirty minutes later we received a call in the guardroom, to say he was causing trouble in the NAAFI, the guard commander and a couple of guys went off to sort it out but the NAAFI was right across the other side of the camp. A few moments I took a call from the

NAAFI saying Stone had gone to the Sergeants mess as he wanted to harm the RSM and was extremely agitated. The sergeants mess was just around the corner from the guard room, so I took the whole guard and sprinted off as fast as we could go. As we neared the mess, Stone was just marching up to the door.

I dived and rugby tackled him bursting through the door and together with the guys, ended up sitting on him in the doorway of the mess anti room just as the occupants were just getting up from their formal dinner. Picture the scene, myself and five other guys were holding down Stone who was shouting and swearing, threatening the RSM and all the other warrant officers.

After explaining we managed to get him back to the cell in the guard room and resumed duties. At eight o'clock we had to take him to the battalion headquarters, by nine fifteen, he was in the back of my land rover with two guards on the way to the station, discharged, de kitted and on his way home.

What a sad and strange guy. These days he would have been identified as an 'at risk' person picked up by the mental health teams.

I was in the Air Cadets from the age of thirteen and learned to fly gliders at RAF Manston together with several hours of Chipmunk trainer flights. When I was old enough to have a moped, I was on standby for flights on weekends when units didn't turn up for one reason or another.

I kept in touch with my detachment commander Chris Nelson, as the garage where I worked serviced his car. One day he called in and asked if I was interested in taking part in an air sea rescue exercise the following weekend. The guy in the air cadets had had second thoughts and he needed a new lunatic so thought of me!

Chris knew I had recently joined the TA so I was technically military. I arrived with the other unsuspecting chap to the air sea rescue unit at Manston bright and early on the following Saturday where we received a safety briefing about crash landing in the water in a helicopter, a further safety brief regarding the exercise and then we were given immersion suits.

We were taken to the harbour in Ramsgate and taken by the lifeboat crew out into the sea somewhere off Deal. We were put into a rubber raft and instructed to pop a flare after the lifeboat had disappeared. We duly let off the flare and waited.

The sea was quite choppy and after a few minutes we both became nauseous, how on earth could people survive for days in a raft, I had no idea. After several minutes of feeling awful the helicopter appeared in the distance, although it was a well-planned exercise, we were very pleased to see it heading towards us but it veered off and headed out to sea.

We popped another flare and it circled around and came overhead. The winch man come down and put the harness around me and up I went. After a few moments my colleague was winched up and we returned to Manston. The lifeboat returned to collect the rubber raft and that was deemed endex.

The debrief went well and we than all went to the restaurant and had a hearty lunch which set aside the sickness and then we returned to the squadron office. A call came in and the guys were all gone in a flash, a major rescue down the channel was in progress and the squadron was urgently needed, not even time to say goodbye.

Chapter 10

Exercise Eternal Triangle

In 1983 we deployed to the 33 Brigade exercise in Germany in the autumn as usual, the journey to and from the exercise is mentioned in an earlier chapter but suffice to say it was the usual trauma. When I think to more recent times the whole journey from home to Hameln would only take four hours including the tunnel crossing. Back then twenty-four hours was the norm.

Our first week on the ground was build up training basically shaking out under the watchful eye of the brigade staff. I am convinced that they thought we were a bunch of weekenders who knew nothing and were likely to sabotage the major exercise.

We of course excelled ourselves and during the middle weekend we had a few hours rest. During this time the brigade organised a visit to the inner German border to wave at the East Germans in the watch towers.

We were under strict instructions not to make rude gestures to the guards across the wire; we were in range of their AK47's we didn't want to start a diplomatic incident!

Exercise Eternal Triangle was joined and as usual we fitted in seamlessly and soldiered on. During the weekend it started to rain again and became quite miserable and cold.

We were playing the enemy in this scenario so in order to look different we had to wear our 'cap comforters', Light weight trousers and red tabs on our shoulder flaps. We only had one pair of lightweight trousers on issue then, they were similar to the 'cargo' trousers fashionable today.

After 24 hours we became cold and damp right through. On day two we moved the echelon to a more exposed area to the south we were under a bridge of the Autobahn. Initially we thought this would be shelter but it was too high to protect us from the constant rain.

We had some time on our hands again, and as always, the war stories were retold with more embellishment than the previous time. Pete Bartlett was always a good source of a tale, in particular, he re-told the stories in the desert in Libya. The desert was incredibly hot during the day and extremely cold at night. Pete was describing how a 'Benghazi Burner' worked.

He had noticed that the ground under the bridge was sandy. He then started to dig with a spade, revealing a layer of white sand, he then proceeded to empty a complete jerry can of exercise fuel on to it. Pete explained that in firm sand this would burn for over an hour so we thought this was an extremely good plan.

A match was thrown; a huge 'whoomph' and we had a heater. About twenty guys appeared from the trucks and we all agreed our trousers would dry in no time.

After about ten minutes the fire started to produce thick black smoke. After a bit of discussion, we agreed that when the motorway was being built some oil was spilt into the sand and this caused the thick black smoke. What we couldn't see was the effect of this was fifty meters above us on the motorway.

The smoke whirled around and filled the road for a couple of hundred yards. The fire brigade and the police were called by a worried motorist. After a while the sirens became closer. We thought we might be in trouble so we decided to hit our sleeping bags and watch the fun.

Four fire engines and two police cars appeared and there was hell to pay. The commander of the echelon received a good lecture from the police but it was interesting to watch the fire brigade trying to put out the fire. I always thought you had to put foam on a fuel fire, these guys were pouring water on to it so of course it went out. Then it relit once the water stopped. That went on for over an hour!

The next day a brigade order came out banning any fire lighting! I had to go out the next day to collect rations and became lost. The maps we had were very good but they dissolved when wet. I ended up low on fuel at a major barracks. To this day I have no idea where it was.

I decided to call in to try and get some fuel, but the guys on the gate said the fuel point was closed until the following morning. As there was no one around and the camp was guarded by the rear party, they said we could use one of the barrack blocks for a shower and sleep and they would advise the cook house to prepare more food!

The barracks were warm dry and inviting, after a huge meal of steak and chips off we went to have a shower and wash our lightweights. On exercise when you have a permanent vehicle, you always have your kit with you, so out came the sleeping bags and a good night's sleep was had by all.

After a substantial breakfast (after all we had been eating compo for days) we refuelled and set about our task. We managed to scrounge a new map and off we went. When we returned to our echelon, we thought we would be in trouble for being out of touch for nearly two days but to our complete surprise they hadn't even missed us.

When I had booked out the watchkeeper had not written it down. Awaiting me were two new boxes of compo and as we had been out on the road, the opportunity to get three hours sleep! No one noticed how we had clean clothes and smelling of deodorant!

The year after I became a sergeant, I was selected to attend a range management course at the South East Specialist Training Team at Aldershot. The instructors were selected from all across the units in the area. One of the things I had learned early on with the TA, was that if vacancies came up in specialist unit the parent unit would always get rid of the awkward guys not viewing this as an opportunity for people development. This was just the case in the SESTT.

There was a bunch of guys who were getting near the end or their service and in this case, they fitted the mould exactly. They between them had not passed a fitness test for years and they had serious attitude.

We are talking mid 1980s when bullying and general nastiness was still the norm; this was harping back to the national service days of the 1950s and 1960s when the guys concerned were a reluctant army.

We were bullied into passing the training course held over two consecutive weekends, I was then qualified to run ranges, i.e., twenty-five metre indoor ranges up to fixed point ranges such as Hythe and Lydd. Over the years I conducted many live firing exercises and some years later I attended a further course which enabled me to conduct ranges of the next group. The training team were a nasty bunch of guys who had a fearsome reputation; I hoped I would not come across them again.

About a year later I was selected to attend a course for an assistant Nuclear, Biological and Chemical warfare instructor. I was keen to do this course as I had developed an interest in the subject, through sheer fascination over the various training weekends. I was a little dubious about this when I discovered that it was to be with the South East Training Team in Aldershot again.

The same bunch of guys was running the training course with a couple of new guys who were a little less imposing. The first weekend was great fun and having learned a huge amount went back the following weekend to complete the course. The second weekend focussed more on the collective training, and we were going to simulate a platoon ambush in complete NBC kit, to give us the feel of how wearing all this kit, changes the way you operate in an environment where chemical weapons have been deployed. To make it more disorientating it was going to be conducted at night.

After dusk we put all out kit on and drew weapons and awaited the orders. The most unrealistic part of this sadly was the instructors did not dress the part. They didn't even put on the NBC suits to add a feel of reality so we were a little disillusioned and to be fair pretty many of the students switched off during this course.

There was a real mixture of guys on this course, ranging from corporals to a captain from our sister battalion in Horsham. At the appointed start time we received our final briefing and issued ammunition and pyrotechnics. We broke open the boxes and the guys started to charge up the magazines and dish out the thunder flashes and trip flares.

I needed to go to the toilet and whilst I was outside, I reflected on the evening and to my horror I realised that we had been given live ammunition and not blank. Guys were putting magazines on their weapons and this could end in a real disaster.

I rushed back inside the building, removed my gas mask and shouted STOP at the top of my voice. This command was instilled in all of us so everyone did just that. The instructors tried to override the command but I asked them to wait and bear with me. Without explaining further, I asked everyone to line up and face away from me and then I gave the command to 'Unload' Everyone then removed the magazines from their weapons and cleared them.

I went up the line with a torch and ensured the chambers were clear of rounds. The instructors were furious and started shouting and generally losing the plot. I then explained we had been given live rounds and no one had noticed. They protested and tried to give me a hard time saying I was trying to ruin the training and who was I to interfere?

The captain checked the ammunition and put the instructors in their place. I ensured all the live ammunition was put back their boxes and accounted for. The blank ammunition was then handed out but I asked why on earth they had live on such an exercise that clearly had no range stage? This was a question indeed; clearly something was not right here.

The exercise was conducted and I passed the course. On the Monday morning I received a phone call from my unit asking me to put the events of the previous Saturday night into writing, and drop it into the barracks at my earliest opportunity. I did this and thought no more about the incident.

A few weeks later I heard the fascists in the training team had been replaced, a new OC had been appointed and they were advertising for new instructors.

Some of the very best guys in our unit went on to be part of that team and the courses were always oversubscribed. Over the years the Brigade training teams were always staffed predominately with guys and girls from our unit gaining huge amount of respect from all who had dealings with them.

I had a letter from the General Officer Commanding congratulating me on my actions which was really quite humbling; I was only doing my job as a qualified range conducting officer.

Chapter 11

The Elham valley takeover

When the cost of moving the battalion command element to Germany for weekend exercises became prohibitive, more adventurous ways of adding realism were employed. Our battalion area in Germany, the Sibbesse gap was similar in shape with wood lines along the hills and roads in surprisingly similar places.

Our training major at the time entered into negotiations with the local farmers and landowners so we could walk over the ground and site theoretical company positions etc.

We would arrive on Saturday morning armed with map cases and overlays of the ground in Germany and place positions and discuss ranges and targets. We walked around the village oblivious to the local residents who were fascinated by fifty or so soldiers wandering about in their sleepy hollow, talking about siting weapon systems and digging holes in their gardens.

We would all break for lunch and visit the local hostelries. Talk of the effective ranges of MILAN missiles and blowing up trees to block the main road to obstruct tanks, totally bemused the locals.

One of the local residents asked what we were doing, and was somewhat taken aback when told by a wise guy, that we were planning for WW3! We did several study days in the Elham area, the countryside was absolutely perfect as a substitute for the German countryside.

Just recently I did a talk for the local Royal British Legion branch in Elham about being involved in the Cold war. I did ask if anyone remembers the soldiers wandering about at weekends, and many of them did. I did let on that in fact it was a cost cutting exercise, and the Elham valley was far cheaper than sending all the battalion hierarchy to Germany for the weekend!

Several TEWT's/study days were held over a couple of years until our role changed and the Sibbesse gap no longer featured in our training plan. The Army went to great lengths to provide realistic training areas in the UK to simulate the German countryside.

There were villages built in Thetford, Salisbury Plain, Otterburn and near Catterick to look like any one of the thousands we had taken over during our time in Germany. They looked identical and were a perfect place to add the realism needed without transporting everyone abroad.

The first one was completed in late 1989 just in time for the fall of the Berlin wall and the end of the cold war era and deployments to Germany. Such is life!

Chapter 12

Ambulance driving in the Medway towns.

In the first training weekend after Christmas in 1987, there was the final range weekend to qualify for our £800 tax free bounty. Everyone had to attend and pass this test annually to get the cash. The weekend was organised as a mop up to capture all the stragglers for bounty tests.

This particular weekend was so cold; we arrived on a Friday night and drove down to Hythe ranges. We settled in and after breakfast we drew our weapons from the armoury and hopped onto the trucks.

I do recall wearing 2 pairs of army green long johns, looking rather like a frog and with a huge civvie jumper on, waddled to the ranges. I don't remember it ever being colder, the sky was dark grey and a northeast wind blew constantly, it even found a way around the corners.

We did our eight mile fitness test that weekend along the range roads, but I did have the sense to remove jumpers and 'long johns' before we started. We were back in Canterbury after lunch on Sunday putting away the vehicles. We remarked that it looked like it would snow anytime soon.

There was always an air of satisfaction after these weekends as the annual bonus, a tax-free bounty would now appear in our bank accounts on or around the first of April. Just as we were getting into our cars a few flakes of snow began to fall from the leaden and heavy sky gently settling on the windscreen.

The following morning, I awoke to the news the Medway towns had sustained twenty inches of snow overnight, and the road networks and infrastructure had ground to a halt.

I struggled into work that morning not looking forward to standing around in the cold all day doing estimates for body repairs for the unfortunate people who had sustained damage.

Around midday the telephone rang, and Pete Bartlett's voice asked if I could get a few days off as of now. The civilian authorities had requested assistance from the military, and we were to deploy our four-wheel drive ambulance to the ambulance station in Gillingham to assist the existing paramedics.

My boss at work thought that I could be released so by mid-afternoon I was on my way to Gillingham ambulance station.

The civilian version of the emergency vehicle was only two wheel drive and with all the specialist kit in the rear, was very unstable in snow hence the need for our vehicles.

We were welcomed with open arms, we were briefed and then settled in to their processes and routines. We had not worked with the civilian emergency services since the 1970s during the miners' strike and it was to be a new experience. We had to arrange feeding via the hospital canteen, and refuelling locally at the fire station.

The paramedics went home at the end of their shifts if they could, but some of them were from some distance away and stayed in the ambulance station. We set up camp beds in the rest room and arranged a shift rota to match the permanent guys. After a few hours a few more paramedics arrived.

They lived locally but couldn't get to their normal work places due to the weather so they pitched in with us. We had three ambulances with two drivers with each. At any one time there would be two ambulances on standby with the third held in ten minutes readiness. The paramedics moved all the kit to our vehicles and set up the oxygen etc.

The military drivers all had some experience of first aid and some of us had attended a course arranged by our medical officer, working in the A&E in Canterbury hospital to give us experience in first line first aid. It turned out this was an invaluable part of our training, for what was about to happen over the next week.

The weather worsened and sometimes a minor issue at home becomes a major problem through fear, uncertainty and the weather closing in. The knowledge of you being unable to get the car out and drive to the doctors or hospital increased the calls to the ambulance service through these reasons.

Conversely the fire service next door saw very few call outs, luckily, they had some four-wheel drives on site which was able to cope with their needs over the next few days, and we were able to call on them when needed. We conducted familiarisation training so we knew how to get to the hospital in Gillingham, the paramedic of course would be in the back during an emergency call, so unable to give us directions.

I started on the second shift so was able to get some rest. When it was my turn to be on call, I realised that we would be rather on our own. The radios were mounted in the cabs of the normal ambulances and we of course didn't have any. Once despatched it was ten pence in the phone box!

On our first call I was paired with a paramedic called Julie, she lived fairly locally and a young mother of school age children. I guess she was about ten years older than me and it was clear she was a very experienced paramedic.

Our first call out was a house in Chatham where a gentleman had a suspected heart attack. I drove with the blue lights flashing down Chatham hill. This hill had the steepest gradient in the Medway towns. Driving cautiously, I slid and slipped my way to the bottom and headed up a small side street.

It was just about three in the morning and cars were parked on both sides of the road, this would have been a tight squeeze without the snow and it was extremely difficult to get through without hitting a car.

On arrival at the house, we abandoned the land rover in the middle of the road and I helped Julie carry the kit to the house. The owners said the father in his late 50s was unwell in bed so we lugged all our kit up the staircase. The stairs had a sharp turn just a few steps from the top. Julie did her stuff while I watched her and passed her bits of kit upon request.

It was clear after just a few minutes of being on site that this guy had indeed suffered a heart attack and needed to go to the Hospital. This was where it now became problematical; he was 57 years old and weighed 26 stone. He was huge! The chair we had for moving immobile patients was useless because he was so large, he would not fit in it.

He couldn't walk properly at the best of times as evidenced by a wheelchair on the way in so we were stuck! Even with the help of the family we couldn't move this guy out of bed let alone down the stairs. We used the house phone to call the ambulance station; this was years before mobile phones were available to everyone. After some discussion they felt that it was pointless sending another crew as we still wouldn't be able to shift this guy.

I remembered that the Gurkhas had soldiers on standby to assist with the shovelling and helping people in the remote areas so we called Kitchener barracks guard room. Fortunately, they had a platoon in on rest break and they agreed to send out a section of them in a four-ton truck. Kitchener was only a short distance away and after about fifteen minutes they arrived.

Julie was getting nervous that the patient was deteriorating and was becoming concerned for his wellbeing. On top of this the family could see we were having difficulties which lead them to become upset. The other ambulance arrived from its call out with an A&E doctor on board with some specialist kit.

The doctor and the two paramedics worked on this guy to stabilise him whilst I passed bits of kit and held a drip. After a while it was decided by the doctor that we had nothing to lose by moving him. We wrapped him in blankets and his duvet and the Gurkhas picked him up complete and we started the difficult task of getting him down the stairs.

This was so difficult as he wouldn't bend in the right places, the doctor was trying to work on him by his chest, I had the drip by his head and the whole scene was like something from a movie. We were stuck solid, nowhere to go, couldn't move him upwards or downwards.

I suggested we get the Gurkhas to lie face down on the stairs and we slid the patient down their backs to the ground floor. Once we had overcome the language barrier (not sure what lie face down on the stairs in Gur Khali was!) This seemed to work and the humour level increased.

We loaded the poor guy on board together with the doctor and the two medics and after I shut the door, the family became a little shirty they couldn't ride with the patient. I explained there was not enough room and the Gurkhas agreed to drop them at the hospital in their truck.

Some people are just not grateful; we had spent the best part of two hours struggling to keep this guy alive in the worst weather for a century not to mention the harrowing saga of actually getting him into to the ambulance and they wanted a lift!

We had still to negotiate the hill in Chatham going the other way. The doctor asked if I could drive as quick as possible as the patient was on his way out. We eventually arrived at the hospital some thirty-five minutes later totally exhausted. The staff were waiting and offloaded the patient, working on him before I had even released the securing straps. Julie and I cleared up the back of the vehicle, restocked the kit and went back to base exhausted.

When we arrived those around applauded Julie on a job well done. What an introduction to the world of the paramedics. We barely had time to go to the toilet and have a cup of tea and we were off again. This time it was even more complicated.

A woman had gone into labour and rather than call an ambulance, the father had decided to drive his wife to the hospital. Unfortunately, on one of the roads near the dockyard there is a sharp bend on a downward slope.

The poor guy was driving too fast on the hill and ploughed into the parked cars, catapulting off at a right angle into a van coming the other way. The impact was about 20 mph, so quite a bit of vehicle damage occurred.

This was not the problem, once on scene, we had four casualties, the two workmen in the van were not wearing their seatbelts and quite badly injured as a result. The car driver had broken bones and probably the most importantly the woman's labour had gone into the final stages with the shock of the impact and concern for her husband's injuries.

Julie went to the guys in the van whilst I looked at the occupants of the car. The driver clearly had broken his right arm and right leg; the bones were sticking out but had not pierced the skin. The woman was screaming but through childbirth pain not injury as best as I could establish.

I asked a passer-by to call the fire brigade asking for cutting equipment. The snow became worse and a white out occurred which was very disconcerting.

Julie was unable to assist me as her patients were also in a bad way. She called out instructions and asked questions regarding the childbirth. I followed her instructions whilst immobilising the driver's injuries.

The seat of the car tilted backwards almost flat so I was able to get her to lie flat whilst I reached across and splinted the drivers arm and then his leg, all the while listening to Julie's shouting.

By now we had several bystanders and the poor girl was becoming hoarse! Eventually the driver was stable and the fire engine arrived and began cutting the roof off the car. I was inside with the patient and eventually the baby was delivered. I placed the baby on the woman's chest and covered them both with a blanket.

I was covered in blood, all over my face and all down my combat kit. Once the roof was off the firemen helped me carry both patients into the ambulance. The weather was closing in again. In the back of an army ambulance, you can wind up the bed frames to make four beds.

We loaded the mother onto the bottom bed and strapped her in and the father to the top one and did up the belts as best as possible so not to interfere with his injuries. After a few moments Julie's patients were lifted in and secured and I began the journey to hospital.

By now the population were about trying to get to work and the traffic jams were building. Although we had a very loud siren and flashing lights no one moved out of the way. Everyone for themselves I feel! The siren was a single note which in the 1960s was the norm, as always, the army use technology that worked when they purchased it decades ago and saw no reason to update it. Budgetary controls were always paramount! Eventually after what seemed an age we arrived at the hospital.

Once we had unloaded everyone, topped up on basic supplies and called base, we had a welcoming breakfast at the canteen. The eight hours shift we had just done was in fact nine and a half, we were off duty but instead of a meal in slow time we had to rush back to hand over the ambulance to the next crew.

Julie went home and I had sixteen hours until the next duty. I hit the sleeping bag and slept for ten hours. While I was asleep the guys had taken my blood soaked combat kit to the laundry around the corner and it was all cleaned for free, the locals were really grateful we were supporting the local community.

After a trip back to the hospital canteen I was ready for my next shift. The guy who I was paired with this time was Mark. He was a senior paramedic normally based in Lewisham but living in Gillingham had gone to the station just up the road to report for duty.

We attended a series of calls, some serious and some complete time wasters but the shift was quite uneventful. I then had a further sixteen hours off and by the next time I reported for duty the dynamics of the weather had changed.

The snow had eventually stopped and the clouds had cleared. An icy wind howled down from the north and the frost was unbelievable. All the major roads became black ice and moving around was almost impossible. Even standing up on the pavements was fraught with problems.

The majority of calls were broken bones and accidents from falling and tripping up. We did have a further heart attack but this guy was in his car and easy to deal with. Mark taught me how to put in a cannula and fix a line which came in useful the next day.

The A&E department had become overcrowded with people and some of our team, were redistributed to assist. The off duty paramedics who couldn't get home and some of the first aid trained military personnel all pitched in to help. Outside the medical problems there was a huge queue of broken bones, general illness, and hypothermia cases etc which were dealt with our team.

We spent sixteen hours nonstop until the queues diminished. I became very adept at using gas and air and applying dressings and wound management. I even removed a single Lego block from an ear of someone who should have known better!

I visited the lady who I helped give birth and she and the baby were doing fine. She asked what my name was and apologised for getting me messy! I have my suspicions there is a lad around thirty years old called John living in Chatham!

I discovered the big guy who had the heart attack on my first day didn't make it. He died about an hour after we got him to the hospital. I did feel a bit guilty over this but we couldn't have done any more. Some years later through work I had to call at the house next door to look at a car. While I was there his wife came out to go shopping but she didn't recognise me.

About a month later I was getting in my car to go to work and there was a car crash at the bottom of the road about one hundred meters away. I rushed down there and another woman was in labour in the badly damaged car. Everyone else had minor injuries but the mother was the priority. I remembered the training I had from Julie and successfully delivered a baby girl before the police and ambulance arrived.

The woman asked if I had ever delivered a baby before and very nonchalantly replied I had and she was in safe hands. I handed her over to the ambulance crew and I headed off to work a little blood stained but walking on a cloud.

A few weeks later everyone who was involved was invited up to the ambulance station in Gillingham for a thank you party arranged by the hospital. Everyone who was not on duty was there and we had a great time. Some really great people work in the

NHS system in the Medway towns and I was quite sorry I lost touch with them all.

This period heralded the increased working relationship with the civilian authorities which evolved into what it is today. The working relationship with the military today is much more integrated and structured.

Chapter 13

Skill or gamesmanship

Later in the year we entered a national driving competition which the best of the best usually went in for. Our unit had entered the first team in many years. I was to command the team with my driver Bob Vidler in the land rover and the 4-ton truck had Eric Bushell as the driver and Harry Cook as the vehicle commander.

We felt we had an advantage as Bob and Eric were probably the most competent drivers in our unit. Harry was a dour guy, he had been in the unit years before joining the regulars, but after his twenty-two years contract, had re-joined us and was made MT corporal on his first day back. Harry knew all the tricks and was an asset to any unit he was with. Sadly, since the first edition was published Harry is no longer with us.

The competition consisted of two rounds, all the units in the district could provide as many teams as they could, perform the type of tests and obstacles to the best of their ability and the first five teams would then go through to the annual defensive driver competition at Leconfield a few weeks later.

The type of tests was quite varied, from basic driver tasks such as wheel changing, fault finding (dead easy this one, both Eric and I were trained mechanics!) Overcoming obstacles with bits missing etc, together with map reading, convoy driving, route planning and time trials both cross country and on the roads around Aldershot.

Our team did quite well and was second on the board at the end of day one. Clearly there were some complete muppets on this weekend so we thought we would turn an advantage in our favour. The first test in the morning after breakfast was a time trial to a part of the training area where would be scored accordingly. If we were either early or late points would be deducted. If you drove at an average of twenty-six mph over the ten-mile course you would end up at zero points. This was good as the minimum number of points won the day?

We identified the competition and the guys who didn't stand a chance and did a bit of interfering. On a Bedford truck there is a fuel turn off lever right by the fuel cap, a swift turn to the right killed the fuel supply after about a mile and the vehicle would grind to a halt. Once you had turned on the tap the engine would take about two minutes to suck through enough fuel to start.

Just before breakfast we nobbled the trucks belonging to the good teams and left the numpties vehicles as they were. If we had nobbled everyone's we would have been excluded so careful planning ensued. We set off in the finish order of the previous day, we marked up our maps and planned the route and waited for our start time.

At exactly 09:10 we crossed the start line and the trial began. About a mile down the road, we passed the first team by the side of the road with their hazard lights on, a breezy wave and before we knew it, we crossed the finish line and waited for the others to arrive.

Bob though it would be a good idea if we then turned off our tap so if anyone complained we could counter with' Look someone has messed with our truck!' completely indignant looks with plenty of huffing and puffing!

When the stage was completed, the problem was flagged to the marshals but they said as it was random, they couldn't pin the crime on to anyone. Bob then started to moan about our truck being sabotaged! An Oscar was on its way. We won the competition and took our trophy smugly looking around at the other competitors, who certainly were not magnanimous in defeat!

Two weeks later with a padlock securing the fuel tap to the 'on' position we were off to Leconfield. Canterbury to Leconfield is around 340 miles, in a 4 ton truck the most you can achieve is forty five to fifty miles per hour so by the maths, it is a long and tedious drive. We left Canterbury mid-afternoon on the Friday and arrived in East Yorkshire well after ten pm.

A welcoming meal awaited us and we hit the sack. After breakfast we attended the briefing, there were teams from all the brigades and districts, together with teams from Germany and SHAPE in Belgium so the competition was stiff. Of the thirty plus teams we were only one of two TA teams so the pressure was on.

We did the same sort of tests as previously with some variations but in the main, it was the same. Oddly the timed road drive was early on the Sunday morning so having identified the opposition who stood a chance we went to work again.

We were about half way down the movement list, and bade our time by double checking the directions and map route etc to ensure the details were correct.

When we left the road had vehicles scatted at intervals, clearly, they had not been wise to the tap trick and it seemed only a couple of us had padlocks on our taps!

We arrived exactly on time and got the maximum score. At the presentation we were a modest third behind two very expert teams from Germany. It was then mentioned that we were a TA team and had barely practised at all. The regular teams had been practising for weeks! We took part in similar events over the years but never as well as the first one.

We went back to Canterbury and arrived very late in the evening on the Sunday, just ready for home and work the following morning.

We entered a team the following year but didn't achieve nearly as high a result at Leconfield. We did get the chance to look round some new kit that eventually we would see as the regulars had some as cast offs!

Chapter 14

The serious stuff

When I was promoted to Warrant Officer, life became a little more serious, as second in command to the MTO decisions regarding major road moves, logistics and greater tactical awareness came across my desk. I say desk loosely, as my 'desk' was an armchair in the corner of the office with a notepad on my lap!

At the same time, I left my job in the garage and joined one of the larger insurance companies as a vehicle assessor working from home. This gave me more scope to work with the TA team in Canterbury.

Part of my new army responsibilities was undertaking the BAOR tick test in the company outstations which meant travelling all-round the home counties in the evenings after work for a couple of months to ensure everyone was qualified to drive on the continent. This was quite onerous as I used to get home well after midnight having not left Guildford until ten pm.

I had to liaise with the chief clerk to get the vehicle load lists correct for the Customs on both side of the channel. Load manifests were a complete pain because not every vehicle had on board what it was declaring, things were always being swopped around at the eleventh hour.

I became responsible for driver training and licence acquisition and used to put together a combat driving course every couple of years to get soldiers through the various licence groups needed, together with teaching the dark art of cross-country driving, camouflage and concealment and navigating across Salisbury plain after dark with no lights.

This was always a busy period. But it was done very professionally with qualified instructors and driving examiners.

The first week was devoted to licence acquisition and the second we deployed to a training area complete with weapons and full kit. We taught the students how to replenish after dark, how to hide a 4-ton truck in a wood, and this of course even harder in a town to achieve.

Convoy driving, was important training too as everyone had to know the basics. Anti-ambush drills were quite fun, we had thunder flashes and blank ammunition in abundance.

Occasionally we had other vehicles to gain licence groups. We sometimes borrowed coaches from the local transport squadron and gave the drivers a hard-earned category D licence or an unusual vehicle to convert drivers to.

My role on exercise was to be the second in command to the officer who commanded Headquarters company at A2 echelon. He used to attend the brigade meetings daily to deliver resupply requests and get the latest tactical updates.

My role was to keep the echelon running tasking the daily resupply runs, be responsible for the defence of our piece of Germany and to be a watch keeper on the radio.

As EU laws were shaped and integrated into the army several things had to change which had a direct effect on drivers and soldiers as a whole. From the front-line soldier's perspective, the most laughable and indeed ludicrous thing to be imposed on us was the portable toilet.

For many years you used to dig a hole with your entrenching tool and then backfill when you had done what you needed to. This happened from the time when the Roman Empire expanded and roads were built to the far corners of their empire. If you needed to go you dug a hole!

EU rules stated you could no longer dig a hole to go to the toilet; in fact, you couldn't even pee behind a tree! So, Wolfgang's brother had to deploy bright blue toilets to your position. You were not allowed to camouflage them so it was always a giveaway of your position.

During busy exercise periods you would see hundreds of flatbed trucks hurtling around the countryside collecting and delivering the Turdis's. They were given this nickname because they looked like the time travelling machine of Dr Who fame.

Because of German efficiency they had to be ordered 3 days in advance. The speed of the exercise usually ran in 2-day cycles so it was a bit of hit and miss as to whether these things were in position. I spent my exercise going backwards and forwards from the brigade logistics guys to our Commanding Officer, badgering him to let me know his thought on where he intended his companies to be placed in three days' time.

I knew more about the battalion's tactics than his own Operations Officer! Mostly it worked unless the brigade changed the plan but usually there were six toilets waiting for a company to tactically infiltrate a wooded position. If Wolfgang's brother couldn't read a map, we simply moved where to the toilets had been abandoned!

Behind my back I was known as the Bogmeister, a rather harsh title I feel but I suppose upon reflection it was very apt for the time.

EU rules also dictated that the exemption to the driver's hour's rules was no longer valid; this caused us many problems in the early days because you had to train double the drivers plus more. You had to stick to the tachograph rules which in many ways was completely nonsensical, how can you train for war and then have to have a fifteen-minute break after four and a half hours driving? To make matters more ridiculous the working time regulations also were brought in, which sometimes stopped us completely for twelve hours.

When the CO wanted to do a battalion move, we simply couldn't do it. No matter how much huffing and puffing was done we had to wait and rest. This had a knock on effect where drivers were unable to do guard duties, dig trenches they just had to sleep. With limited man power this really caused friction, the non-drivers had to do all the work which clearly doesn't seem fair to those guys.

1989 was a momentous year for the world, the imminent softening of relations between the Soviets and the West came to fruition and for us the last full scale BAOR exercise although we didn't know it yet.

In the September we deployed to Westminster Barracks in Minden. Clifton barracks next door was the home of 2 Queens one of our regular sister battalions. I drove out on the road party in a 4-ton truck.

My co driver was Henry Thomas; he was the battalion's chief clerk, a regular soldier who had just joined us from 2 Queens! It seemed rather ironic that having just arrived from Clifton barracks a week earlier he was on the road back to Minden with us! I worked with Henry for many years after this, more on this later.

The brigade we were serving with was already out on exercise so the two barracks were remarkably quiet. The first few days were settling in and doing warm up training etc. A battalion party was held and during the next day we prepared to deploy on exercise.

This particular year for the first time I remember we had completed the return journey paperwork, other than the ferry booking. The assumption was I believe that as we came in from the exercise a day early, we would undertake this paperwork with the help of our regular counterparts next door.

The exercise was joined and all went well. The woods we deployed to were in a very hilly area. To make life a little more difficult it rained all the time. One of the memories from this period, was at night driving down a small road in a 4-ton truck hundreds of huge frogs were hopping down the wet road illuminated by the headlights. We had to stop and move them out of the way to avoid running them over!

The echelon where we were based at this time was in a reverse slope of a wood and radio communications was non-existent. We were unable to move as the area we were using belonged to local landowners and the days of simply taking over a farm or a wood were long gone, so we were stuck.

We had an arrangement with the commander of A1 echelon that he would send a runner in a vehicle to advise us of troop lifts and resupply needs. We did have radio communications with the brigade on the admin net but nothing forwards to the troops on the ground, battalion headquarters or A1 echelon. As exercises go this was a pretty boring one for us, we camouflaged our vehicles and settled into a routine.

The company positions were static as I alluded to earlier so vehicle movement was minimal. In fact, we didn't behave tactically during this period, other than a signaller and watch keeper in the command post (who must have been so bored without any radio traffic) and two guys on guard to just be security the remainder slept in the back of the trucks.

At this point I will just mention the capabilities of our radios. The standard VHF radio used in vehicles could have a range of 20km but they were affected by terrain, atmospherics and weather conditions.

They were designed with the plains of Germany in mind as that was their intended place of use but in reality, they were unreliable and sometimes just useless. You could be talking at maximum range one moment and the next an adjacent station 200 meters couldn't hear you.

The long-range set worked on the HF band. This set was designed for much longer distances and worked well when talking to station 200 miles away but again you couldn't speak to the next station in the next village. I suppose what I am alluding to is the radio communications in that era where not reliable.

During this quiet period, we sent some of the guys back into camp for showers as we knew there was no movement for thirty-six hours, the A1 echelon and the rifle companies were due to move but we didn't know the new locations. It was felt by the commander that we should stay put and wait for orders but at the same time he sent me out in the command vehicle to try and establish communications with the battalion.

After about an hour, I managed to make contact under my own callsign, and was immediately ordered to proceed to a specific grid reference to meet up with the commanding officer.

This seemed a little unusual to receive an order such as this out of the blue so my mind was working overtime wondering what I done and the need to go directly to the CO.

When I arrived at the battalion headquarters a very sombre mood was everywhere. I was ushered into the CO's tent to be advised I was to take command of the return to the UK, the transport officer and one of the REME guys had been involved in a serious road traffic accident.

Bill the MTO was supervising the battalion move at a road junction in the early hours of the morning. The whole idea of wearing combat clothing was to not be seen but unfortunately on this day the world changed for Bill Gawler our MTO. A driver came along at speed; we believe he was a doctor on a call out and although he drove around the stationary vehicles, he hadn't seen Bill or corporal Green from the REME. Although health and safety was purveying through the army, reflective vests to make your presence visible were not yet issued.

Bill was taken to hospital in Hannover with some serious injuries, indeed it was deemed so serious that his wife was flown over from the UK to be with him. The REME corporal was not injured too badly and was released a couple of days later. Bill stayed in hospital for over a month before being well enough to return to hospital in the UK.

My task was to return to camp and organise the return home. This was fraught with problems, the people I needed to liaise with in the UK had gone on leave and their counterparts in brigade were out on exercise. Perhaps it had not been such a good idea not to complete this paperwork before we deployed! After a sleepless night and hours on the telephone the task was done.

The road move was not uneventful, as the guys loaded up their kit it became clear that far more vehicles than usual would not start. Despite the best efforts of our fitters, we still struggled to get everyone started. After the recovery trailer was loaded and trucks attached to dead vehicles by rigid bars, there was one land rover still dead. We towed it round to the workshops of the battalion next door to await their return from exercise.

The journey was slow and tedious back to Dunkirk, the weight of the towed vehicles slowed the convoy down and at the first rest stop I decided to split them up and send them off in one group. When we reached the ferry, I completed the paperwork and just as we boarded the slow-moving vehicles arrived with minutes to spare. We didn't see the broken down land rover again.

The spares needed made the cost uneconomical to repair. This was unfortunate as the land rover was one of the battalion command vehicles which due to the nature of its specification, was almost impossible to be replaced.

Oddly years later the ordnance system replaced the vehicle and we drove to Hilton in Staffordshire to collect the replacement. This turned out to be older than the one we had lost and as always with the army; the law of sod was applied. The next day we received an urgent signal to prepare four vehicles to be sent to the docks near Southampton for deployment to Bosnia.

This newly arrived vehicle was one of the registration numbers allocated for this task! We never did have it replaced, shortly afterwards our scale of vehicles was drastically reduced and we entered another era.

Our battalion headquarters was involved annually in a major exercise in Germany. It was essentially a desktop exercise with all the brigade unit headquarters and A1 echelons set up tactically in an old Wehrmacht barracks. The brigade headquarters was set up tactically in a farm about ten kilometres away.

My role this particular exercise was to stand in for the officer commanding HQ company who on exercise was the battalion logistics officer. He was responsible for the resupply of the battalion. It was going to be a desktop exercise using notional figures.

We all were fed centrally in a cookhouse set up by our sister battalion 2 Queens. We knew many of the key people from our previous soiree to Minden.

I was not needed at the beginning phase so it was arranged that I would fly to RAF Gutersloh on a Friday evening and be collected by Darryl Key, our permanent staff REME guy who was in charge of the management of repairs within our battalion and taken to the exercise location.

Our Adjutant had a bit of a sense of humour; he advised that I should wear a suit when travelling and being the gullible sort believed him. I turned up at RAF Lyneham in my 3 piece suit with all my kit looking as sharp as nine pence.

The RAF guys were laughing like drains, Hercules were they only aircraft at Lyneham at that time which was the RAF equivalent of a 4 ton truck! After take-off I endured ninety minutes of sniggering while wearing the ear defenders to drown out the noise of the engines and the mickey taking, then landed at Gutersloh. I vowed combats would be worn on the return journey.

I joined the exercise, rolled my suit up into my Bergen and reported to the CO. I had to attend the daily conference at brigade headquarters normally at ten o'clock in the morning, to update brigade on our resupply needs and to be advised of the latest tactical situation. This information was then given at the CO orders group later in the day.

I was told to be at the back gate at 9am every day where I would be collected. Everyone in camp was clean with well pressed clothes and not a weapon to be seen. I arrived at the back gate at 08:50, tooled up, helmet and webbing complete with camouflage cream and a borrowed pistol.

The guard arrived and unlocked the gate no transport was there. I thought about it for a few moments and surmised that if a vehicle was taking me, we would be going out the front gate. At that moment a Lynx helicopter arrived, I boarded and had the thrill of a lifetime, the pilots were bored as we ground hugged all the way to brigade headquarters! Scared me witless!

We arrived at headquarters and the pilot said he would return in two hours; with that he was gone. I attend the conference, took the relevant notes and marked up the map had tea and then returned to the helicopter. Again, we hugged the ground; the pilot asked if I had to be back at a certain time, I responded no so we went on a tour of our old area in the Sibbesse gap and all around that area which evoked so many memories from our Cold War days.

The guys were green with envy when I explained what had happened and they kept asking if I needed someone to come on the following day to carry my kit for me! No chance I enjoyed a week of this personal transport!

The following year our battalion was asked to participate in a TEWT (tactical exercise without troops) at the battlegroup trainer at Sennelager. The whole of the battalion headquarters was to deploy and all kit was packed ready to go but two days before the deployment, it was announced that due to cutbacks only two guys could attend.

One of these was the OC of HQ coy for logistics who couldn't go due to work commitments, and our training major to act as an umpire. I was asked to undertake the role of OC HQ coy, having recently done it in Germany so after a bit of quick packing I was ready to go (wearing combat kit this time!)

Off we went to RAF Lyneham again, this time in combat kit. There was a delay in the flights and we were bumped off the next few flights as high-ranking officers had a higher priority, yes that was understandable as rank does have its privileges. We couldn't work out why the lance corporal and his search dog were a higher priority than us.

We finally arrived at Gutersloh two days later and then had a wait for a further day for transport to Sennelager. They had given up waiting and gone home for the weekend! We arrived at the TEWT forty minutes before it finished so went to have breakfast and within the hour, we were on our way back to Gutersloh. A most economical use of government money!

Chapter 15

The adventurous driving examiner

I ran the platoon after this for about a year and during this time I attended a driving examiners course at the School of Mechanical Transport at Leconfield near Hull.

Leconfield was an old RAF airfield used during WW2 as a base for bombers. It was used to train driver and maintenance courses, driving instructors and driving examiners, together with conversions to new vehicles to the army. It was an area I knew well; I had attended a couple of competitions there together with an instructor's course some years earlier.

The station was approximately two miles from the old market town of Beverley. I suspect as this was the nearest place you could get a drink from camp so the locals would be bombarded with soldiers on a nightly basis. The town square had a structure that looked like a bandstand with a large horse trough in front, on a nightly basis a van would appear there around 8pm selling the most delightful homemade pizzas. This was always welcome after a couple of pints.

We all used to have a large meal in camp prior to either walking, or catching a taxi into the town; I can't imagine the number of calories we used to get through, but we were young and very energetic. We were also sober; the two miles walk back to camp and the half mile to the billet once through the gate soon sobered us up.

The examiners course was very intensive with more than a 50% failure rate with very few courses held during the year, so I consider myself very lucky to have been selected. One advantage was automatic membership to the Institute of

Advanced Motorists as we were considered competent and above the test standard to join.

I qualified for the car and HGV certificate but when they arrived many months later you can imagine my surprise when a motorcycle one arrived too. At this time, I didn't actually hold a full motorcycle licence. All three are still in the frame on the toilet wall! Part of the course was to continually test each other so for two weeks we drove perfectly which became habitual.

I never dreamed I would drive an articulated truck to that standard. At each stage you were tested and observed by two instructors, sometimes a Department of Transport supervisor would accompany you as well to observe the standards are being maintained. The car test seemed the most intensive; I guess this was because the provisional drivers were new to the road whereas the truck or bus learner drivers have already road experience.

The car test was uneventful and then we moved onto the trucks. This was conducted in a Bedford 4-ton TK with three seats. The instructor/examiner sat in the middle whilst a second student was in the far left seat. The style of testing was a little different as the student on the left tested the driver and vice versa. We did complete tests from the reversing exercises on the square to the road drive.

We got to know Hull and Driffield quite well by the end of our time there. The guy in the middle watched and said nothing until the end where we were individually debriefed. This was where the 'walk of shame' occurred. If your buddy had effectively failed, he would go back the sergeants mess, pack his kit and leave. This was known as RTU (Returned to Unit).

Inevitably the individual was so gutted after all the hard work you really didn't get a chance to say goodbye as the instructor always debriefed the guys who had failed first. The decisions you make whilst driving could get you failed and equally if you made a decision or didn't intervene when a dangerous situation was unfolding in front of you.

On my final test I thought I had blown it by stopping the test with just a couple of miles to go back to camp. We were driving along an A road but in a very rural area. My 'student' was doing very well but as we rounded a bend there was two horses and riders, side by side.

He didn't seem to see them and didn't slow down. Twelve thousand things went through my head and as we became closer, I knew I had to act. I said in a loud and commanding voice please stop the vehicle. This seemed to jolt him into a reality check and he pulled up straight away. I followed up with 'I am terminating this test in the interest of public safety and I will drive back to the test centre'

The look on this guy's face was daggers and when he got out of the cab to come around the other side, I slid across to the driving seat inside the cab. We drove back to camp in stony silence; I was praying I did not make any errors as the examiner was sitting quietly writing furiously on his clipboard.

When we parked up, I did the failure sheet as prescribed and went through the debrief and standard wording etc. The student was asked to stay in the cab and I was sent to the office. I was absolutely convinced that I had been too harsh and thousands of what ifs went through my head. I made a cup of tea and waited for my turn to come. It was the last test on the last day, so I was going home anyway after two hard weeks of testing and training. What a way to finish!

After what seemed like an age the examiner came into the room without the other student, I thought that's it failed, how am I going to explain this to my commanding officer, thoughts of wasting tax payer's money and having a bit of a jolly on an easy course went through my mind. The examiner sat down and the first thing he said was well done for terminating the test, done at exactly the right moment based on the facts and potential hazard.

You could have knocked me over with a feather! The examiner went on to say that he was pleased with my actions and how I kept calm and carried out the abort procedure exactly by the book. I had passed the course and I was a fully-fledged and qualified testing officer!

The other guy had admitted he dozed off and was long gone by the time I returned to the mess, twenty students started the course and six passed out at the end, what made it sweet was out of the twenty on the first day, I was the only one from the TA, the rest were regulars!

I stayed a further night in the mess as I couldn't drive home on the Friday night because of the distance and in the bar the stories of the horse were being regaled already even though none of them were there! I kept quiet and smiled!

When I was retested 3 years later, my test experience was still being talked about as an example of how to behave when facing such a hazard!

Because driving examiners are a rare breed, the local driver and testing agency at brigade were very keen to get all the licence groups on to your licence. Once I had done a few tests for them they arranged for me to get the other groups within a few weeks.

I was sent to Chatham garrison to take my group H test; this was the track laying vehicle test in other words a tank! I did not know what to expect never having driven a tracked vehicle.

The relief was felt when I saw the vehicle that I was to be tested on, it was a DN3270 probably the smallest digger in the world to quote the advert. All I had to do was drive it forward and backwards then back the way I had come. Passed, what a result.

I then took the examiner on a coach test. Reciprocal passing completely unethical! A few weeks later I was given the task of doing 2 group H tests for the REME unit in Deal.

The tiny drill hall there is long gone and all that remains is the army cadet hut and a housing estate of the original TA centre. I received the paperwork and off I went. When I arrived, I was greeted by a Scimitar, a light tank made of aluminium and could travel at 60 miles per hour! The driver sat in the front and the commander sat in the turret i.e., ME!

I had never been in one let alone knew how to drive one of these beasties. The REME had to be able to drive all the vehicles they could repair hence the testing. I walked round it and gave it the once over, I found the electrical cut out switches and made sure the tracks were attached to the drive sprockets but what else could I do? I gave the aura of knowing exactly what I was doing but I had never been near one of these in my life.

We did the reversing without any issues then I climbed in, put on the headset and said 'follow the road ahead unless I ask you to turn which I will do in good time' Off we charged out of the gate and off to Deal seafront, all the tourists were shocked to see us, as I was sticking up out of the turret, I had to look cool and completely in control.

Luckily, they couldn't see my legs doing my duck impression. Crikey was I flapping, I had no control of the vehicle; the only contact with the driver was the headset. I kept my cool and vowed I would never do this again until I had done a driver's conversion course.

I never managed to do this so felt I was missing out on something; I quite fancied driving one of these on a cross country training course. The next time I was in an armoured vehicle commander's seat was on patrol in a Warrior armoured fighting vehicle in Kosovo some years later, but more on this further on.

Doing the testing was fun and very lucrative. TA soldiers are paid by the day, my civilian job was home based so I had the ability to juggle my workload to cover any tests needed by brigade. This of course meant double pay, happy days!

I conducted tests for the Junior leaders at Shorncliffe, The Gurkhas in Chatham, my own unit and many others amounting to over 1000 tests. Some notable incidents occurred in the six years I did conducting tests.

Early one morning I received a call asking if I could do a test on an articulated vehicle at eleven am that morning, luckily, I was working in Ashford that day, and so I was able to fit the test in on route. Because of the sometimes-ad hoc nature of testing I was allowed to undertake this in my suit so I didn't have to change into uniform.

My contact at the headquarters was called Vicky, she was a little cagey about this test and after some cajoling I managed to find out that this test was a bit out of the ordinary.

Getting vocational licences through the military was quite an expense to the public purse. In our unit we had to justify the cost of this activity. We had to put a return in every six months with the number of qualified drivers we had for each vehicle type.

This of course changed frequently due to people leaving and others being promoted out of a driving role into a non-driving post.

It was very unlikely officers would hold a vocational licence; they rarely drove and certainly not trucks. The only exception to this was the MTO and occasionally the QM. When we wanted to conduct internal training, we had to apply for funding to cover the training days well in advance.

I mention this because the test I was asked to conduct involved a senior naval officer. Somehow through using influence and contacts he had managed to get his group D coach licence and his group C rigid lorry licence. This had infuriated the staff at brigade as clearly this was a little dodgy. The other tests had been done some months earlier and had been fraught with problems.

Admiral A*se as I will call him had failed both these tests first time and registered formal complaints against the examiners. He then had to be retested by the most senior examiner in the brigade known as the Master driver. He passed both tests by a whisker and complained that the other two examiners were useless and should be struck off. I knew both of them well and they were very competent examiners.

Now it was my turn, Admiral A*se had managed to get permission and a vehicle to take his C+E licence to drive an articulated vehicle. This was a different kettle of fish to a coach and rigid. He demanded to be tested by the master driver but had been refused because this then caused a problem if he failed. Another master driver most likely from Colchester would have to come down and deal with the test. I was given the job; they built me up saying I was the most cool and unflappable of the examiners on the team, obviously the horse incident was still fresh in everyone's mind.

I arrived at brigade at 1030 collected the paperwork and headed out to the manoeuvring area where matey was standing looking at his watch! I was ten minutes early so I don't know what the fuss was about. I introduced myself and he immediately questioned my ability to do the job and wanted to know my rank etc. A very unpleasant character!

We started the test and he was useless at the reverse exercise and finally scraped a pass on the third and final chance. We pulled out of the camp gates and started down towards Sandgate, I did feel uneasy at his style of driving and he was making schoolboy errors all the time. My marking sheet was covered in ticks and I wondered how this was going to pan out.

As you go down the hill to Sandgate the road follows a gentle left hand bend downhill. This guy hardly used his mirrors and he was getting closer to the kerb with his rear wheels.

Half way down the hill was a bus stop with a glass shelter, there were a few people walking down the hill but quite a few waiting for the bus which was following us. He picked up speed and mounted the kerb with the rear wheels far too close to the bus shelter. After running the kerb for over one hundred meters, I stopped him and terminated the test.

The shouting and bawling that followed was unbelievable, the sustained rudeness I had never experienced before and it was quite unnecessary. He wanted to know who my CO was and my unit, but when we test, our unit is deemed as brigade headquarters.

The brigadier was from my cap badge so I felt I would be treated fairly (for what I didn't know) I refused to drive him back to Shorncliffe so I called the master driver to arrange a lift. Admiral A*se was collected by his staff car and was in the brigadier's office when I returned to the driving office.

I debriefed the master driver and as I concluded the phone rang summoning me to the brigadier's office. There are two sayings used widely in the army, interview with coffee – that's good! And interview without coffee – that's very bad! I wondered what was coming!

The PA in his outer officer raised her eyebrows and smiled in a knowing way. I knocked and was called to enter. The brigadier was sitting at his desk on the telephone; he motioned me to sit in an adjacent armchair – good sign! And his PA brought in coffee and biscuits – very good sign!

Brig was speaking in a very firm manner about my new best friend and after about five minutes of one-way conversation he put the phone down and came and sat opposite me.' How's things with you RQ?' (How did he know what my next posting was going to be, I didn't at that stage?) Could be a bit better I responded, I had a most unusual experience today.

Brig asked what happened and when I explained that Admiral A*se almost took out a bus shelter and three young mums with push chairs. He stood and shook my hand and congratulated me on my quick thinking. Brigadier John Holman MC was a fine and much respected officer from my own regiment, the Queens. I had met him a few times when he was a colonel but this was the first time since had taken up the appointment. He leaned over and called his PA to ask if Admiral A*se could come into the office.

He arrived about five minutes later and entered the room without knocking to see me biscuit in hand; drinking percolated coffee laughing with the Brig.

Brig stood up and told admiral in no uncertain terms he would never drive a military vehicle again. He had just spoken to the CGS in Whitehall and after the explanation would be summoning the Admiral the next day. Something to do with abusing public funds etc! He then said I want you apologise to your examiner for your childish behaviour, this is RQMS Bennett (no I wasn't yet?) from one of my battalions a fine and respected individual.

I accepted the apology and the chat afterwards formed part of my commissioning interview unbeknown to me! The next time I saw him about six months later we were on exercise in Thetford, he pushed past the officers and came over and shook my hand.

I offered him a cup of coffee and we sat on the bumper of a land rover and had a chat for about fifteen minutes. The CO and entourage were hanging about moving from one foot to another waiting for Brigadier John to finish with me so they could start the visit program.

Brig John asked if I would consider commissioning to fill the gap left by Bill Gawler which I accepted but due to technicalities was a further two and a bit years before I took up appointment.

After the visit the CO asked what had happened because Brig John had not discussed this with him previously. Very embarrassing!

Shortly after this event I agreed to undertake some driving tests for the Gurkha company attached to the battalion at Howe Barracks. I did many tests that week and on completion they had a party for everyone involved. Gurkhas can cook the most amazing curries and true to form we had a curry meal laid on for us.

This consisted of fourteen courses, some of these curries I had never seen before let alone the ingredients. It was polite not to ask what they contained but a few were quite obvious, sausage curry, chicken, lamb, beef and goat curry, but some were very difficult to identify but delicious beyond belief!

The Gurkhas don't drink alcohol so the variety of soft drinks quenched and cleansed the palate between courses. Many of the base ingredients had been sent over from Nepal especially for the event!

I enjoyed working with the Gurkhas they had a wicked sense of humour and a good command of English despite acting sometimes a little dumb! The Engineers in Chatham ran several courses and I did many uneventful tests on both car and truck.

Over a few weeks I did numerous tests on coaches and to this day you see Gurkhas, long retired, still driving coaches for military contractors and local bus companies. I felt I had to resign from the role as driving examiner when I commissioned as the young soldiers were intimidated by my commission. The young soldiers couldn't relax with an officer conducting tests.

One day I was due for a formal interview with the CO, these happened annually where you received a progress report and debrief on your previous year's performance. I was happy in my skin and comfortable in my job, I was expecting to stay where I was for a couple more years but without me realising, I was holding up 3 other promotions.

The CO advised that I was in line to be the next RQMS but someone was being posted in course qualified so I had to wait for a couple of years. I was unsure of my next move; I wasn't keen to go out of the battalion as it was widely known at that time, once you were out it was unlikely you would come back.

Chapter 16

Typewriters, bullets and bombs

The CO suggested that I took up a vacant post in the orderly room as the Chief Clerk. I agreed and ended working for Henry Thomas who I mentioned earlier. Henry understood that my post was somewhat reluctant but he was a great teacher. He taught me to use a word processor and then a computer and gave me the time to learn to type.

In the orderly room Henry worked with Ken, a retired sergeant from the Royal Green Jackets who joined us on a uniformed civil service contract who was his deputy. Ken had a dry and wicked sense of humour, a fantastic guy who brightened every situation.

With him was the finance warrant officer Jim Reynolds, Jim joined us on the same type of contract as Ken from the brigade team at the end of his 22-year regular engagement. Jim was a Scot, who had the driest humour I have ever known, again a great guy whose attention to detail was bordering on obsessive, a real credit to his skill and training.

We all worked well together and made a great team. I did not deploy on exercise anymore, I stayed in the orderly room as an emergency contact for the guys on the exercise. I waved the trucks goodbye on a Friday evening and saw them back on Sunday afternoon.

During my time in this job, I perfected my typing and collated the regimental archive from old exercise instructions found in boxes and old filing cabinets. It took a couple of years but I managed to get a complete history of exercises and annual camps for 5 Queens from the amalgamation in 1966 to date.

In 1987 we deployed to Wathgill camp near Richmond in the heart of Yorkshire, after a long drive and working into the evening to set up the battalion orderly room we went to bed with instructions to report with marching kit at 05:00 for a battalion shake out exercise.

Having done no military training for a while clearly, I needed a plan. It would not look good if the third most senior warrant officer had to fall out and spend the long drive home in the ambulance!

All the participants kit had to be weighed to ensure that the correct amount of weight was carried, you had to have a certain weight to pass the combat fitness test. This exercise counted for this test so guys were adding sand and heavy bits of kit to make sure they qualified. I arrived late just as it was about to start, made sure my name was taken, missed the weigh in and started the test!

This was the hardest fitness test I had ever taken; the pace was ferocious and soon guys and girls were falling out by the side of the track. I was running up and own encouraging the guys, positively sprinting and making sure all the important people saw me in action.

The last half mile was hard even for me and I was quite done for at the end. We all had our names taken again and that was that. We had breakfast at 07:30 and carried on at our first day of camp.

I went back to my room and removed the puffed-up sleeping bag from my bergan and the bubble wrap from my pouches. Bennett has a backup plan at all times!

Later in the morning whilst I was typing up the exercise instructions, I noticed the CO and his Adjutant had left their bergans next to my desk. I picked them up to put them into the CO office and lo and behold they contained sleeping bags!

Bloody cheats! I took the Mickey out of the Adjutant which counted against me in due course; he made me suffer when I went through the commissioning process but again, more on that later.

I spent three days conducting driving tests to still keep my hand in and still be able to avoid the final exercise by being in the orderly room with Henry and the others. I learned a great deal during this period but I did feel guilty not deploying with everyone else as that was what I did best.

Wearing barrack dress and working all day in an office was not really my bag. I enjoy sleeping out under the stars and doing proper soldiering. When the opportunity came to take the appointment of the Regimental Quartermaster Sergeant (RQMS), I would be comfortable in this role, I had done the accounts course some years back and this was one step up from that. I also have a technical background which certainly helped and had done my range management and field firing qualifications a few years before so I understood how the accounting system worked for ammunition.

I did my course at Backdown Barracks and learned the art of completing an AFG1033 to a high standard using a ruler! These days this is all done on computers back then it was all paper and in duplicate! Filling in small forms correctly even down to the correct date format. We were all a bit fed up with doing this for two days but a little after returning back to my unit, it dawned on me that this was designed to instil an attention to details.

Unlike normal stores, you had to have an extremely high accuracy rate; bear in mind one round of ammunition unaccounted for could be used by a dubious character on the streets.

I settled into the job well and although a little daunting, became the second most senior warrant officer by appointment.

By default, I also became the president of the warrant officers and sergeant's mess. As they say, the bigger the badge the bigger the responsibility.

The first year was quite uneventful; I deployed on exercises, accounting for ammunition and was involved in range weekends. Early in the second year we were advised we would be going to Thetford to Wretham camp sharing facilities with our sister battalion 6/7 PWRR.

It became apparent that due to the plans for ranges and the type of ammunition used we couldn't keep the ammunition in the small bunker in the camp complex. The nearest storage facilities were 25 miles away so just wasn't practical. We were mulling the problem over in the office in Canterbury with the quartermaster, Dave McCaig the solution presented itself.

At the back of the largest field firing range in the Thetford training area is a place called Frog Hill. Never heard of it you say? You may not have heard of it but you would have seen it many times on BBC TV. The opening and closing sequences of Dads Army were filmed there!

Behind the firing points was a road leading to Wretham and behind this on a gentle slope was a large flat field about ¾ mile squared. In front of the firing point the ground gently slopes downward and you can see uninterrupted views across Norfolk for about 3 miles.

This is interspersed by wooded areas, many ranges designed for some of the heavier weapons, field firing ranges and a short runway used for short take off and landing exercises with Hercules aircraft. There is a river where you can practise tactical crossings and a bailey bridge which covers a pond. It is believed it has been in that position since 1943.

Some of the villages have been converted to buildings to train soldiers in urban warfare; latterly a whole town was built to mirror the style of houses in Germany where we had spent so much time. I applaud the authenticity but the year it was completed the Berlin wall came down and the look was not needed anymore! This village has also been on BBC, you may recall Top Gear have used it a few times over the years.

During the summer months there is a plethora of wildlife including Barn, Tawny and long eared owls. At dusk the air is full of Nightjars catching flying insects. Thetford training area was invoked by the military in WW2 to train for the allied landings, all the villages were emptied and residents displaced.

Their descendants are allowed once a year to return to the home villages for the day. Also, on occasions the churches hold special services but these add up to no more than 3 per year. This also applies to the villages of Imber on Salisbury Plain and the farms and hamlets at Sennybridge in South Wales.

The area has virtually no light pollution and apart from the area at Sennybridge you get the most marvellous view of the stars when it was not raining. Thetford was always my favourite training area right back to the late 1970s in the days of 6 Field Force!

You could drive off in a land rover for fifteen minutes and once you had switched off the engine and the lights, you could be anywhere. So peaceful, just the sounds of nature around you. I first heard a Nightjar in the Thetford Forest with its distinctive clicking of its wings and purring noises permeating through the dusk.

So back to the field behind Frog hill, this area of flat ground was perfect to build a field storage ammunition cage. We sought permission from the brigade HQ and in response they sent a set of plans to build the beast.

We demanded razor wire, pickets, generators and tentage from the system. The assault pioneers were tasked to build this and off we went. The advance party to annual camp usually deployed 2 days before the main body, but in this case, we left for Thetford on the Tuesday, just over four days before the battalion arrived ready to train.

The reason for the early arrival was to ensure the rations, ammunition and accommodation was in place, together with recces of ranges and training facilities etc.

Our sister battalion 6/7PWRR were sharing the main training camp with us and it therefore made sense we also shared the ammunition compound. When the facility was complete it was a very secure compound, the only way in was past the tent where the guard lived. They were there 24/7 until we had used the ammunition.

We had a very old 1950s marquee which was erected to keep the ammunition dry, 6/7 kept theirs in the open exposed to the elements.

We had borrowed a combat fork lift to unload the ammunition from the four articulated trucks, checking batch numbers and distributing between the two units took all day and then into the night to finally check the quantities.

The fork lift was called an Eager Beaver, absolutely hilarious name for a vehicle but it had the same cross-country capability as a 4-ton truck so it was no lightweight vehicle. It was articulated and open to the elements, although you could drive it on the road, it was moved by trailer over distances more than a couple of miles as it jumped about and made the drive feel like riding in a small boat in a storm, and often made the driver physically sick!

On the first full day of camp, we were up very early and at the compound to issue the ammunition, after a while the range teams arrived and it became very busy. At this point it became clear we should have built the compound a little larger. The guys from the other unit arrived at the same time blocking the gate with their vehicles and causing sheer uproar. The ammunition was issued and I settled down for the day. I did a stock check and all was well, I bade the guard goodbye and went for a drive around the training area.

I went to the old bailey bridge and had a look around. This hadn't changed for decades; the pond now was surrounded by mature trees and because of this undertaking river crossings had to be done upstream. I recalled the time a very good friend of mine suggested we went fishing, we were in position nearby and the food was getting a little boring.

We were doing a week of range packages and very unusually, we were in a tactical hide rather than in barracks. Jack tied six thunder flashes together and then to a brick. He struck the fuses and threw the bomb into the river. After a few moments there are a phzzz and that was that. Jack was disappointed and vowed to increase the explosion.

Two days later we went fishing again; unbelievably Jack had hidden a grenade in his kit and again tied it to a brick, pulled the pin and threw it into the water. A huge plume of water erupted and as the water settled, we saw one of the training area staff coming down the road in his land rover. Obviously if we had been caught, we would have been in serious trouble, mainly for stealing a grenade but also ruining the commanders fishing stock.

Clearly the warden had not seen or heard the misdemeanour and as he went over the bridge, he must have seen the trout floating on the water. He was out in a flash, up to his waist and scooped up the lot! What a pain, we went back to the hide and had a tin of beans and went to bed.

I was told that this trick was done again in the lake at Pippingford Park but sadly there were no fish in the pond at all, frogs, newts and eels but nothing edible.

In the late afternoon the range teams started to drift back in with empty cases and ammunition boxes. The damaged and unused rounds were handed in and I closed the account for the night. My colleague on the other side of the compound was still beavering away; I bade him a good night and headed to the mess for supper.

The next day the previous day's events repeated themselves. But on the second day I became concerned, after everyone had gone to the ranges my stock check was wrong. I had some 64000 rounds of 4BIT extra to my stock check of the previous day.

4BIT is the acronym for 4 ball and 1 tracer, used on night shoots to indicate fall of shot out from three hundred meters. These extra two boxes had the same batch number as the ones I already had in my stock. Very odd, in particular since I hadn't issued any! I reported the fact to the QM who also thought it was a little odd, he agreed to do a stock check and sign the sheets accordingly. This was done just after lunch and signed off accordingly.

That night there was a night shoot and more 4BIT was issued and very little was returned. Again, a check was done and I headed for bed. In the morning I issued the ammunition as before, this time we had some 66mm anti-tank rounds that had a date of 1962 on them. We had been asked if we wanted them as they were the last ones in the system. We agreed but ordered extra demolition kits in case we had to blow them up if they didn't work.

This day there wasn't any field firing ranges, it was all antitank 9mm sub calibre spotter rounds and grenades etc. I did my stock check and to my astonishment I had two more boxes of 4BIT. I telephone the QM who came straight out to the compound. He agreed that I was correct and then it dawned on us.

The guys across the way were always counting and checking. Clearly, he couldn't count! At the end of the day, he ended up with extras and he then sneaked them across to my pile! You can't bring extra ammunition onto charge too often so I was asked to give it to the range teams without any paperwork. Even if they didn't want 4BIT they got it!

Late that night we sat away back with night vision goggles and watched him do it. When he was confronted, he admitted his error and he received back a stack of boxes and after that all was well. This episode cut down on my bird watching time so I was a bit miffed.

I was asked to go to the range where the 66mm rockets were being used and as predicted they didn't all go bang! After a few misfires and fizzes, we decided to blow the whole lot up. We took four at a time, packed them with plastic explosives and attached the detonator cord and walked back, getting undercover just as they blew up. This was a tremendous explosion, much more intense than a grenade going off.

We must have paid the Americans a fortune for them back in the 1960s and here we were, giving the government value for money! This was a bad year for misfires; we had to stop throwing grenades as there were so many blinds, we ran out of plastic explosives.

You always have to have a demolition kit if you are using grenades. So, what to do with ten grenades? It's very difficult to backload them and you can't store them in a normal camp facility so they were becoming awkward.

Our numerically challenged friend across the way was doing his checks and I noticed a demolitions box in his pile. I asked if I could borrow it and we took all the grenades out to the middle of the ranges late at night and blew the lot up! He had the cheek to complain we had used too much explosive and not enough detonator cord. Easy, cut off a chunk and throw into the bin!

On the last day of the range package, we had fired enough ammunition to have very little left in stock, careful husbandry had meant that any remaining, could go back to camp ammunition store and remain within the allowed licence category. Our friend across that way didn't have that luxury; he missed his day off sitting in a field on a pile of boxes.

All the next week he was trying to offload ammunition to units coming up the following week! On the exercise in the second week, we lost a guy, he was unaccounted for so a major search was actioned. Because we practised all sort of scenarios the operation was smooth and eventually, he turned up, charged and sent home!

In the last year as RQMS we went to Kielder Forest in Northumberland. We had an uneventful time until someone else went missing. This was worse than the year before on the open area of Norfolk, this time it was close forest and it took 3 days of wasted time to find the guy. As it happens, he was found by someone not looking for him! A guy was doing a chip shop run and spotted movement next to the road.

The forest was quite a unique place; the woodland was managed incredibly well, although the MOD used it as a major training area it was managed by the Forestry commission. During the exercise we were harboured up along a track, as usual with Northumberland it rained constantly, the wet woods absorbed the sounds but seemed to amplify the noises of the wildlife.

Sounds of raptors during the day echoed around in a most eerily way, at night the sounds of the long-eared owls pierced the night together with the usual tawny owls hooting to each other made this area a very strange experience for the guys who would normally live in a town where these noises were completely unheard of. It was quite funny to see guys in their 30s looking nervous at the sound of an owl!

Chapter 17

How to get a commission the hard way!

I finally commissioned in March 1996 after jumping through all the hoops put in front of me. It seemed that although they wanted a commissioned MTO they didn't think it should be me. At that time some of the senior officers within the battalion didn't rate my abilities. I complied with every request to go through the processes, I am sure they made it harder so I would fail.

I had to go the Aldershot for a second commissioning interview, this time with a board of three senior officers. I passed this with a good score, then I was then asked to go to Westbury to attend the selection and boarding weekend. I passed this successfully, despite being nearly twice the age of my contemporises.

One incident which stood out was the injury of one of the directing staff on the confidence course. He was standing too close to a log swing, one of the guys jumped on it but it shot sideways and hit the guy hard on his temple. He went down like a stone and the medics didn't have a clue how to deal with it. I took charge and organised an ambulance etc. Again, not quite the normal day in the office!

I passed the course and was advised I would be commissioned in about a month. When you commission from a senior warrant officer you generally go straight to captain rank but not me. The adjutant, at the time didn't take to me and put as many obstacles in front of me as he could, hence Westbury and the second interview.

He applied for 2nd Lieutenant for my rank; this is only given to young officers who have just passed Sandhurst. I complained vehemently to the commanding officer and lieutenant rank was duly applied for.

I was not happy but when I found out I was getting a category A commission I was pleased to bits. Category A commissions are awarded to post Sandhurst and ex ranking guys normally get what they call a Cat B or QM's commission.

Category A commission opens doors and you are treated exactly the same as someone who has gone through the sausage mill. As a consequence, I was qualified and able to do any of the jobs given to me and even was qualified to attend Staff College and achieved a B+ grade, not many officers in my unit had ever done that well, late entry or not! All things considered not bad for a guy who missed over half of his primary school education and went to a school in the middle of two fighting communities of miners.

Most of my time at secondary school was wasted by police visits, brawls and searches; I don't think I did too badly in the end!

When I returned from my obligatory 2 weeks leave after I commissioned, I reported to the new CO, Robert Knight who just said go and be my MTO, a man of few words was Robert! Shortly before annual camp that year in Belgium he called me in to his office and again in a few words promoted me to Officer Commanding HQ company for the duration of the exercise. After all he concluded, I would have the smallest company and the current incumbent was needed to command the rifle company in Gillingham.

That two-month period building up to the camp was incredibly busy, not only had I to do the paperwork to get us to the continent, I had to plan a field firing range and take over the duties of OC from the previous incumbent.

The rifle companies were deploying with forty five guys each but given we had attached chefs, signallers, fitters and drivers, HQ company deployed with one hundred and twenty guys! So much for the smallest company commanded by the least senior officer in the battalion! I handed over my duties when we arrived to my warrant officer, Bob Vidler.

Bob had always been one rank behind me as we had progressed through the MT and when I commissioned, I was pleased to recommend him for immediate promotion.

We also learned that we had a detachment of 666 Sqn Army air corps attached to us. One of these gazelle helicopters was for my use! Even the CO didn't have his own chopper!

The range package I had been planning was cancelled due to the ranges being broken from a previous unit. I was a little disappointed because I had great things planned. It was a defensive shoot based around a building, if it had come off it would have been very impressive.

The infantry platoon would have been in defensive positions inside; the machine gun platoon would have had an SF gun set up on the roof to suppress the 'enemy' infantry out to 1800 meters. The 94mm antitank weapons would be either side of the building to take out the oncoming tank targets and finally the infantry would engage at three hundred metres. All this was to be conducted at night, very challenging for the troops concerned.

I busied my time in the first week with barrack duties and dealing with all officer type things. The company busied itself with its normal duties and this would have happened without my interference. Every day I visited the troops, tea with the Signals platoon, a brew with the REME and a catch up in the MT office.

The RQMS was doing his stuff together with the QMs department. I did a couple of recces for the exercise in the second week, primarily to give the pilots air time and guys experience flights. A Gazelle only had one pilot in the right hand seat, the senior passenger on board sat in the left hand seat but the controls had been removed to give plenty of space for a rifle and kit.

Behind were seats for a further three guys but it was a tight squeeze. Behind them in the tail section of the fuselage was a storage area. We looked at a wood to prepare for moving in, we flew nose on sideways all around the entire round the two kilometres square wood at two feet off the ground. This was the most comprehensive recce's I had ever done. What a strange experience.

One of our command land rovers broke down and needed a spare part. This was not available locally so a telephone call was made and we arranged to pick up the critical part from the distribution warehouse in Donnington! The pilot of my helicopter jumped at the chance and made a couple of phone calls to secure air traffic control clearance and a refuelling stop.

Darryl (Jeff) Key the REME sergeant was up for the ride so with paperwork in hand off they went. Six and a half hours later including a stop off at the workshops in Canterbury to get some other parts needed for non essential repairs, they were back in Belgium.

Yet again another useful exploitation of tax payer's money but I guess it would have cost more to recover the vehicle back home via civilian contractor, plus the workload of removing the radio kit, probably vaguely justified our use of the helicopter!

A ten pound brake cylinder probably cost £4k to collect! Two days later the REME needed another part, this time the only one available was at Rheindalen garrison so off he went again.

A study day was held on the Friday prior to a day off in Arlon on the Saturday. This was very educational as it covered the American 101st airborne activities in 1944/1945 following on from the encirclement of Bastogne which of course is well documented. We walked the woods above some of the objectives they attacked and defended. The defensive positions were quite visible on the front of the wood line.

Some of our junior officers were quite frankly not taking this seriously. They were messing around and one of them kicked a lump on the ground. This stopped everyone in their tracks. The lump was an American helmet which rolled across the wood. The spade symbol was still very obvious painted on its side; this was the unit symbol of the 101st. The liner was still intact and this was a significant find.

I guess the helmet had been covered by dirt during a mortar or artillery strike, and after many years had been pushed up by tree roots on the ridge line. I often wonder if its owner survived this dark time in our recent history. The helmet was snaffled safely away as a significant trophy.

I arranged transport for the guys in the company down to Arlon and spent the day in camp. I walked around the ranges and generally had a relaxing day. I also did a bit of pre work on the exercise and although I had done the job of OC HQ Coy several times over the years as a warrant officer, I had never done it wearing the badge!

We deployed into the forests and for the first two days, the battalion didn't need us so we used the helicopter to practise casualty evacuation. The camp was ten minutes away by air and a useful opportunity to do low level training. Bob Vidler was bitten by a mosquito and due to the nature of the 'wound' we evacuated him back to camp for twelve hours!

This gave valuable practise to his sergeant who stepped up to do his duties whilst Bob was away. Bob duly returned smelling sweet and looking very clean in his pressed combats. I confirmed with battalion if we would be moving that night and having been given a 'no' dispatched the helicopter armed with company funds to buy burgers, rolls, salad and loads of beer from the supermarket.

Visualise the scene, a gazelle helicopter circles above the surprised shoppers, lands at the back of the car park, followed by a pilot in his flying helmet pushing a trolley around the supermarket as if it was completely the norm. The evening was very pleasant, a warm breeze meandered through the woods and it was a very peaceful evening. The radio operator remoted the handsets for the radios and we chilled out round a small fire telling war stories!

The next day I was called to an orders group with the CO, now being a bit of a cheeky guy, I decided to utilise the helicopter, everyone else arrived either on foot or by land rover but Bennett turned up in his helicopter. Knowing how the CO operated I had a word in his ear to the effect that if he handed over command to his second in command, he could take a ride back into camp, for a shower and hot meal before coming out later that evening before last light.

The CO flustered and blustered saying it was a ridiculous idea and I should be ashamed for even suggesting it, and by the way I shouldn't abuse the helicopter as it made the other company commanders jealous!

The orders were delivered for the next phase and we knew what was in store for us next. Just as it was finishing the CO announced he had to visit brigade HQ for a meeting and he was going to cadge a lift with me. He handed over command to the 2ic, winking and smiling at me, and away we went. The CO dropped me off at the echelon and off he went to his 'meeting'

The return journey took its toll on the battalion vehicles, many had to be collected from the roadside and towed to the docks, fortunately our recovery trailer was empty for the return journey and had to be used to collect one of our command vehicles. It had been shunted and rolled down a bank by a civilian truck.

Luckily Steve Hughes and Chas Oliver were unhurt although battery acid burnt holes in their combat kit. Canterbury was littered with broken vehicles for months after this. The availability of vehicle spares had reduced again, and it took months for even the simplest things to be available through the military system.

Chapter 18

Okehampton, second time around

The next camp we attended was a military skills and field firing training period on Dartmoor. This was to be a far simpler deployment than in 1979 but it was complicated by the battalion having to exercise the freedom of Ramsgate on the first day. So, with most of the battalion heading towards Ramsgate in coaches the green fleet was hastily heading in the other direction to Devon.

For the first time I decided I would travel down by motorcycle. We had Harley Davidson's by this time, electric start and a real pleasure to ride. I took a couple of gallon cans of petrol to avoid stopping and off I went. Six hours later I was in Okehampton camp.

The camp hadn't changed but the A38 now cut through the hills around the town. The railway siding was long gone. We had chance to settle in and await the coaches with the guys who had been on parade.

The range packages were to be quite intense so the following morning we issued every vehicle we had, except mine to the companies and range teams. The camp was completely empty by 9 o'clock and eerily quiet. The only guys around were from the quartermaster's department and some of the signals platoon who were checking comms for the exercise.

Bob and I decided to go for a drive around the moor after a cup of tea; we took my land rover and linked in with the signals to check the comms up on the moors.

After a couple of hours, we went back to camp just in time for lunch. Communications around Dartmoor are very much dependant on the weather. On a sunny day comms were fine with both the VHF and HF sets work well going out to quite a range.

If it rained or was misty and dank as it was most of the time, you were lucky if you could get one hundred meters!

The HF set worked very well right out to the furthest end of the range road link, going out to several miles with hundreds of meters vertical height. This simple test would help to save lives later in the week.

On the night before the day off there was some issues with the girls in the female accommodation blocks. I still don't know what it was about but while the investigations were done, I was asked to take the girls involved out of camp for the day. Steve Tompkins came with me as the minibus driver and we headed off to Exeter.

After a nice lunch and a wander around we decided to go and see a film. I was asked not to go back before 5pm so plenty of time. I was given expenses for the day so the army paid for us to go and see Saving Private Ryan which was a real treat in surround sound, and of course on their time. Once again, a good use of public funds.

When the exercise phase started clearly, we couldn't deploy out on to the area as it made sense to be with the infrastructure. We could have set up the command post in the MT office but this wasn't a realistic scenario. We camouflaged the vehicles up on the MT square and assembled the command post in the middle.

Obviously, we didn't need all the drivers to be with their vehicles so we bunked everyone up in the MT office and stores so they could be on call. Other than a driver who was technically a runner/guard the others slept when not on duty. The battalion command post set up on the grass area a couple of hundred yards away from us, and used the same system of manning as us.

Because we were not really part of the exercise, we hadn't drawn weapons so it was quite easy for the guys but that was to about to change.

On the second night the weather closed in and the wind became gale force. The camouflage nets scattered and I decided to remove and store them to avoid damage. To make matters worse the command cell couldn't make contact with the rifle companies who were out on the moors. After some hours, requests started to come through for casualty evacuation for hypothermia etc.

We dispatched the ambulance and a land rover with all the medics to collect them but after an hour or so they returned unable to find the companies. The grid references were checked and clearly, they were not where they said they were.

I went to the command post to see the Operations officer and because the weather was worsening, he decided to wake the colonel. Once the facts were presented, i.e., troops falling over with hypothermia, and the companies were lost it was decided to stop the exercise and bring everyone back in for the night. We would reassess the daylight and see how we went.

The CO asked me if I could find the battalion and I responded that I thought I could. Having been for my drive a few days earlier I had a pretty good idea where everyone was so I said I would go and find them. I checked comms with the command post and took the whole fleet of trucks and ambulances up over the range roads to the top of the hill above the camp.

The rain was horizontal and drove through everything. I put on my reflective yellow workman coat I use on the motorcycle and briefed everyone in the back of a truck where it was dry. I would go forward and search so we didn't lose anyone else and report back to the ambulance that was fitted with a VHF radio who in turn, could relay back to the command post. I radioed forward and eventually made contact with each company in turn as I drove forward onto the area.

I called forward the vehicles in turn and led them to the company positions one group at a time. As the exercise had been cancelled, we drove on full headlamps, where a company was off grid, we also had the hazard lights on plus blew horns so they could get a fix on us.

After a couple of wet cold and miserable hours we had all the battalion heading back to camp, either in trucks or ambulance. The only guys we couldn't find were the recce platoon. I knew that Jack and the lads would be fine and as there were only about twelve of them, they would hunker down and be warm and dry. We had several guys who needed the doctor and were in a bad way.

If they had continued in the bad weather, they would have dropped and been a problem. The doctor advised the CO that the job was done to a high standard, when I returned to camp the CO was pleased to see me and then proceeded to give me a telling off for not wearing military attire! My yellow coat had kept me dry and warm; I didn't care in the slightest! We left the command post for the night and went to bed; the battalion command post did the same except for a radio operator, just in case the recce guys called in for help.

The next morning after the kit was dry the exercise resumed and we dropped off the companies where they should have been the previous evening. The recce platoon appeared having slept the night in a sheep byre, completely dry and well rested! The exercise continued and all then went to plan.

The following evening, I was on duty about eleven pm and wanted to get a ration and ammunition return from the companies. The weather had closed down again, but it was a misty gloom this evening, everything around the camp was strangely quiet as sound is depressed when this type of mist appears. It was like a drizzle but in reality, we were in the cloud line.

Reports and returns are done on the long range HF radios. This was always a bit hit and miss for the companies didn't like using them as they made a loud hissing noise all the time so getting returns was always a bit suspect.

Much to my annoyance not one of them answered my call but on the third attempt a voice came back and acknowledged my call. I asked him to verify his call sign, he came back to me and said his name was Dave and he was on a cargo ship about to dock at the freight port in Durban, South Africa. I had a chat with him for about five minutes and bade him a good day.

I went over to the battalion command post quite excitedly and said to the watchkeeper 'did you just hear that?' They didn't hear a thing; such are the foibles of HF radios. I could talk to guy 5000 miles away but the guy across the square couldn't even hear me!

At the end of the exercise the recce platoon operator came and found me to say he could hear the conversation I had had but try as he might he couldn't get me to hear him.

Chapter 19

End of 5 PWRR and the birth of 3 PWRR

1999 was to see the end of 5PWRR. In the autumn of 1998 in a further defence review it was decided to merge the 5th and 6/7th Battalions. The headquarters was to be at Canterbury and Dover, this was still going to be the assault Pioneer platoon but the other five drill halls were to be closed and sold off.

We were to gain A Coy at Farnham and B Coy at Brighton from 6/7 with C Coy sharing the real estate in Canterbury. Because of the changes in role and the concept of individual reinforcement, the size of HQ Coy was to be reduced significantly and the MT platoon was to lose quite a few vehicles and drivers.

The date of the amalgamation was set at the first of June, a significant day in our regimental history – 'The Glorious First of June' when we celebrate a significant naval battle in 1794 when our predecessors were the first marines to serve with the Royal Navy.

Both the 5th and 6/7th Battalions had a long history with some quite significant achievements along the way, both sporting and military. The old guard saw the merger as nothing short of treason and they vented their spleens accordingly. It was clear that there would be changes, personnel would be displaced and key appointments were to be up for grabs.

I felt that my role was in danger so I made some in roads to finding a job in a different organisation. I knew that there was a guy in 6/7 who was quite highly thought of, would be a threat to me when the decisions were made.

In early January that year the last specialist training weekend of 5PWRR was held. I booked the training area at Lydden where the old ammunition bunkers from WW2 were situated. After a day of driver training, map reading and camouflage drills we settled into the training area tactically. It was a freezing cold day, there had been frost in the previous days and the ground was as hard as rock. We briefed the guys that an enemy attack was due and they should all be vigilant.

During the previous few months, I had asked for blank ammunition, thunder flashes, shermuly's trip flares and smoke grenades. Normally they would question why we wanted so much ammunition but they knew that it was our last weekend before the disbandment.

The day went well and we settled into our night routine. Some of the nco' s set alarms at 05:00 and we then disappeared quietly down the road to a layby. We loaded our rifles, distributed the ammunition and thunder flashes. We then changed into French maid's outfits complete with wigs, false boobs and stockings.

As dawn began to break, we charged back into the compound firing as we went. When we went through the gate it began to snow and instantly our very cold outfits became wet and we were shivering. The lads in defence reacted accordingly, opening up with automatic fire and light and bangs.

We charged about like madmen, shouting and firing and generally making ourselves seen. We used all the ammunition and as the light of dawn started to disclose our dress to the guys. The whole thing collapsed into laughter, the snow became worse and we called all the guys under cover.

I debriefed everyone and explained that the final weekend of the old-style MT platoon was a time to be remembered for a bit of fun not a sad event. After a breakfast and change back into uniform we carried on with the days training. Unusually on our return we went into the junior ranks club to clean our weapons so we could sit around and chat about old times and recount war stories.

The battalion drew down in the early part of 1999 with only low-level training happening after the end of February. We knew the paper establishment so we prepared vehicles to be sent to other units. As always, we picked the 'old dogs' and kept the best as all units do.

When the big day came, I was called into the CO's office and advised I was to be the MTO of 3 PWRR and given the list of guys who would be staying. We lost the responsibility of the MT stores; this was going to be administered by the somewhat reduced REME section.

The rest of the evening was spent doing interviews with the displaced personnel. I do remember it was an emotional time not getting away until long after midnight.

The reality was that this was the end of the old MT platoon that had not changed since I had joined. The establishment of an officer, warrant officer, two sergeants, three corporals, two lance corporals and nine privates were to be reduced to one officer, warrant officer, sergeant, two corporals, one lance corporal and three privates was going to be a shock to us all.

We all, wrongly assumed that any thinning of the platoon would leave the existing members intact but this wasn't to be the case. The old detachment commanders of Guildford and Gillingham joined us which even now seemed odd. Kirsten Andrews lived in Horsham and Steve Tompkins lived in Tonbridge this seems such a long way to drive for a drill night. Ray Wheeler having already been moved to us from Westwood was displaced together with Darren Hance, Steve Reeves, Nick Cullen and Glen Lester all had to leave. They had the opportunity to move to other units but only Ray took this up.

Probably the most bizarre decisions at this time were the displacement of our much-respected company sergeant major, Jack Bright. Jack together with Ray went to 220 Field Ambulance both as corporals. Jack eventually became the acting company Sergeant Major at 220 Field Ambulance just before he retired as staff sergeant.

To say the first drill night after the changes happened was quite tense with the new people joining us and the old guys still training until decisions were finalised. I remember that they only had a month before they moved on.

Later in the year the new battalion went on annual camp for the first time. A field training package and a weeks' worth of drill culminating in HM the Queen of Denmark presenting the new battalion with new colours. At the end of this camp Pete Bartlett retired after many years of loyal service and a new era dawned.

Chapter 20

Exercises in France. Cooperative lantern 2000 and Soissons 2001

I received a phone call out of the blue one day from the battalion asking if I would be able to take an additional two weeks off in June, to attend a multinational brigade exercise in the south of France, Frejus to be precise. Just up the road from St Tropez!

Well do the bears? I asked what job I would be doing and they advised I would be working with media operations, so even better, I jumped at the opportunity.

The day arrived and we boarded the coach for the south of France and sat and snoozed for the next nineteen hours until we arrived in Frejus. There was only one other person I knew on the exercise, Major Richard Long, our battalion second in command, so I whiled away the hours getting to know people.

The exercise was very much like the style of exercises I had attended in the past, and indeed mirrored my time in Kosovo in the years that followed. The composite brigade was made up of Norwegians, Americans, French, Italians, Dutch, Germans and Danish battalions. The exercise director was Brigadier Marcel Valentin, one of the most senior officers in the French army. I met him just a few years later when he was COMKFOR but that's another story!

I worked in the Brigade headquarters, the area was scattered with kerrimecs, metal self-contained offices with plug in facilities ready to go. The media ops cell was a double sized one just big enough to house the team and the computers etc. Our task was to act as if we were on operations and pick up stories, photographs etc and publish a newspaper titled the Daily Lantern.

Sadly, none of these have survived the test of time. We would attend the high-level briefings and pick out some of the more interesting events due to take place both in the headquarters and down to the multinational battalion cells. We also had a gazelle helicopter available to get us to places where the battalions were acting out the serials on the ground. We had unlimited access to everywhere.

After the first day of shaking out and getting to know our team we became heavily involved in interviewing key players and acting out the front-line interviews. The paper contained a mixture of real time information gleaned from CNN which played in the background our office all the time, and the stories we gleaned from our trips out. As the exercise was 24/7, we worked in ten hour shifts with a publication brief with the whole team to decide what should be published in that day's paper.

This was done at 07:00 at shift change over. Where one of the battalions was dealing with a refugee situation we would come up with stories about displaced people and the hardships they were going through to give the exercise players a feel of reality on the desk top exercise.

We published competitions, crosswords and local interest stories etc to give everyone the feeling of a real situation. We were a very disparate bunch of guys; our OC was a Lt Col from the German army by the name of Heinz.

He was a reservist who was employed by a national newspaper, I believe he was related to the family who owned the newspaper. Heinz took to me and I spent many hours in his company and he taught me a significant amount about media operations.

Marcel was a warrant officer from the French army who worked in logistics around the port of Marseilles. He was a little reserved at first as he had some gaps in his English but after the exercise, he was much more outgoing.

We had a technical sergeant from the US national guard who worked in Helm Stadt for the local university. His name eludes me to this day, we did room together and got on very well. He heralded from Los Angeles and even after ten years of working in Europe, he still couldn't cope with the cold weather.

We also had a sergeant from the French foreign legion who was attached to us but he kept his own company. His name was Andy and eventually after a couple of days we discovered he was from Glasgow and probably even now the British Army are still looking for him! He was a bit of a wide boy and obviously wasn't a willing volunteer!

Michael Weitz was a first lieutenant from the US army who had flow over from the states to participate. On the third day I was asked to have lunch with Brigadier Valentin together with Heinz we had a long meeting over lunch and it was decided that the Brig would do a daily media brief on camera and I was to do the questioning.

All the operations cells had a television, and it was possible to broadcast the interviews to all levels on the brigade exercise. Hence, I got to know his ways and how he operated, very useful in the years that followed. The paper was very similar to those published on operations, I am sure this was the case as a few years later in Kosovo a similar publication was issued every day, it followed the format we had adopted.

A week into my tour we were visited at our operations room by the CO of the brigade media operations team, a full colonel named Heinz! A very embarrassing man hug followed and our battalion was visited often after that. One of the guys in the team was a professional photographer whose skills we utilised and produced some very high-quality stills which we were able to use.

We had an observer from NATO who was a negotiator in hostage situations. He decided we were the best place to observe because we always had tea and biscuits in our office. He suggested that I could perhaps join the organisation as a chemical weapons specialist due to my NBC qualification, but I declined to take it further due to home circumstances. This was a good decision as three years later the team spent months in Iraq looking for WMD's.

The exercise was interesting and I learned a tremendous amount of nonmilitary skills during this exercise and on its conclusion, we were able to have a day off before we returned home.

We were transported into St Tropez by coach, and we settled into a bar on the sea front and enjoyed the view. We ordered a beer and then metaphorically fell off the chair, a small beer cost £9, we didn't have too many of these that afternoon!

Heinz wrote to my CO and told him what a good guy I was and how much he enjoyed working with me which was quite useful for my forthcoming annual report.

For my first few years I received annual reports after I had commissioned. These can be useful for those who aspire to military jobs outside the battalion. I was quite lucky with my reports, the first report graded me as a 'B' and the subsequent two graded me as 'A' This I thought would stand me in good stead for future jobs and I was delighted to find out that after only three years I was to be promoted to Officer Commanding Headquarter company.

I was initially to be a captain but I wasn't really bothered by this just pleased to have been given the appointment. I took up the job and settled in but my peers kept jibing me that I was only ranked as a captain.

Eventually I went to see the CO who was by now Peter Jones. Peter was clearly not a fan of mine and when asked was advised I was not senior enough to be a Major. Having served 20+ years, passed staff college with an 'B' grade and been rated two out of three years as a grade 'A' on my confidential reports, I was not having any of it!

The TA system is aligned in many ways to the regular army but it does differ slightly in as much as the brigade deputy commander is always a TA Colonel with manning responsibilities to the TA officers in the officers in the brigade. I wrote a very grovelling letter to Colonel Chris Argent and explained my position.

Now colonel Chris and I had issues in the past. When he was OC HQ Coy, I ended up on top of him at Longmoor when an old railway bed gave way I was driving down. He was squashed up against the side door with me on top of him and I don't believe he ever forgave me for that. Also, he was my CO when I had a Lynx helicopter for a brigade exercise for my use which I am sure ticked him.

I posted the letter to brigade on a Wednesday and on the Saturday, I received a call from Col Chris inviting me to see him in his office later that day. I was not doing anything much so I popped on my suit and drove to Shorncliffe. Col Chris had the biggest office in the building, having been to see the brigadier a few years earlier I certainly could vouch for that!

Col Chris was very displeased that one of his officers was being held back and after a short conversation followed by tea and biscuits putting the worlds to rights and catching up with the events in the battalion, he promised me he would look into the matter. But it might take a few weeks. I was ok with this just grateful to have been granted an interview.

The following Wednesday I received a phone call from our Adjutant asking if I could call in to his office at his convenience which I did the following morning.

He advised that I was now a fully-fledged Major and should wear the appropriate crown before I attended training again. Clearly the CO received a call Monday morning and was brought round to my way of thinking. Thank you, Col Chris, The CO never said a word about the meeting and within 2 weeks I was a substantive major!

The brigade was asked to participate in a multinational exercise in Soissons near Rheims the following year so I volunteered for this as the night shift G4 watchkeeper. It turned out the night shift was extremely quiet so nothing was really learned. One thing I did find odd was the French army have red wine with their evening meal, how decadent I thought!

They also treat the outgoing night shift at 7am as if you were finishing working the evening, so they cooked a full evening meal with the wine and just before you went back to work in the evening you were served breakfast.

Mid way through the night you had a break and received a full lunch in the cookhouse. Talk about messing with your system, I was struggling to cope with working nights without the food foibles! The best bit was a day out visiting a champagne manufacturer Pomeroy! My favourite!

Chapter 21

Countries beginning with K

All TA soldiers ultimate dream is to go on operations with the regular soldiers. In my early years this was all but impossible. The only significant operation during the 1970s/1980s was Operation Banner, the troubles in Northern Ireland. Because this was deemed 'home turf' the TA guys were unable to get involved.

Another factor was the regular army was 120k strong and it was deemed to be large enough to be able to cope with the NI rotations. During this period the battalion was deemed deployable so logistically we couldn't fit in the order of battle on small scale deployments.

We were there for all-out war fighting against the USSR. After the warming of the Cold war some guys with specialist skills went as individual reinforcements to units on operations and this is how my opportunity became a reality.

Our role was changing and rather than the whole unit deploying we were fast approaching the time when platoon size groups would deploy to fill gaps in the rapidly shrinking regular army. In 2002 our 1st Battalion was to deploy on Operation Agricola 8 to Kosovo. I saw an opportunity to be mobilised and campaigned accordingly.

The system was developing a mobilisation centre at Chilwell but they needed to get a full perspective on how the deployment would work for individuals. Our CO was quite keen for me to go as he saw that in the future groups and individuals would follow this path. Iraq and Afghanistan would follow in due course but deployment was still in its infancy.

I was to deploy with the 1st Battalion to work in the operations room, in reality this was a role I had trained for and practised many times so this was not going to be a daunting prospect at all so I felt quite confident that I would be able to deal with situations as they arose.

I found out my shift was to be four pm until eleven pm every day and I was to be given the latitude to be able to get involved in all aspect of the operation outside these hours. This seemed very exciting indeed for the TA officer from Canterbury.

I already knew quite a few guys from the 1st Battalion from the time they served in Howe Barracks prior to them adopting the Armoured infantry role which would ultimately take them to Paderborn in Germany.

On completion of my tour, I was to write a debrief document for the powers to be at Chilwell to assist with the mobilisation process.

The day approached and the softener for me was my employer. They of course hadn't sent one of their employees to war before and didn't realise they were paid by the army. This myth was dissolved with future deployments so I was paid to go to war! In addition to my salary, I would also receive £125 a day to soldier.

Looking back, the grey areas with mobilisations was fine detail behind the pay/pensions etc, where companies stopped paying salaries but this had a detrimental effect on pension continuity. This was eventually resolved with an amendment to the Reserve Forces Act the following year.

Three weeks before departure I attended a pre deployment course with the RAF in Norfolk, I was the only army guy on the course so felt slightly awkward with the hotel dwellers.

The group I was with were the clerks and admin staff from the APOD who only went from their accommodation to the arrivals, hall every day for six months, there were a couple of RAF Regiment corporals who look far older than their rank suggested and a couple of odds and sods whose role I didn't find out.

I didn't let on that I was from the TA so sat quietly at the back. We did refresher training on mine warfare, NBC, first aid, tactics and how to use interpreters. We had various specialists come to present to us over the three days including a very good presentation on conduct after capture.

A practical exercise occurred and the scenario was, we were on a patrol and encountered soldiers from the opposing sides using aggression against us. We were briefed on the scenario and I said to the group if we find some trouble split into two groups and look to see if it was direct aggression towards us or drunk belligerents who perhaps could be talked down.

We had cards with words in Serbian for such events. Off we went and when the' enemy' started firing they all turned around and looked at me for guidance. From the DS perspective this looked hilarious. A group of 20 regular RAF personnel looking to the TA major for help.

I shouted for them to hit the deck and called out the words in Serbian to the effect 'British army drop your weapon' and waited for the response. A burst of gunfire came back and I called again, further gunfire, so I changed tact. I said 'unless you drop your weapons, we will fire on you!' More gunfire ensued so I told the guys on my left to put down covering fire whilst I led the 3 guys with me forward.

We fired and manoeuvred forward until the gunfire stopped. We checked the guys for weapons and papers and radioed for support, while we secured the area. The medic simulated giving first aid and they declared the belligerents were dead, so we didn't have to practise prisoner handling on this occasion.

I obviously made an impression, everyone after this wanted to include me in every conversation and even the directing staff were including me in training decisions. I was laughing as I were sure they didn't know I was TA and feeling pretty smug with myself.

The big send off with flags waving and cheering didn't happen. I was to use a 'one way hire' to get myself to RAF Brize Norton in time for the daily flight into Pristina. The 1st Battalion were already in theatre by about three weeks so they we well in the swing of things.

I arrived late in the evening the day before the flight and went to the departures to drop off my kit. The place was in darkness apart from a dull light in the far corner. A very bored overweight RAF corporal was sitting reading a newspaper and didn't look up on my arrival.

I asked if I was in the right place for the baggage for Pristina he said yes, I was so I was checked in accordingly. The flight was at ten am the next day and he asked me to be back at eight am. I went to the airport hotel which in reality was a transit centre which had recently been done up as families now used the facility.

After a substantial breakfast I reflected on what I was going to be walking in to on my arrival. I had read the accounts of the 2009 build up when the Russians took over the airfield, and General Mike Jackson had to negotiate the standoff with a bottle or two of vodka. I hoped my arrival would be less problematic than General Mike's!

I arrived at the departure lounge which looked completely different with the lights on. It was quite large and recently refurbished. Modern digital flight information boards were in abundance together with TV's showing CNN news. The only flight on the board was the ten am to Pristina, and I was all by myself apart from the same corporal in the baggage area. I enquired whether the flight was busy and he shrugged his shoulders in a most disinterested way.

At 09:30 a civilian crew arrived and checked their baggage. The aircraft in front of the main door was a Boing 737 from 'My Travel' so obviously this was to be my flight. I thought the other passengers were cutting it a bit fine or groups went via another area. At 09:40 two REME technicians arrived without baggage and boarding started immediately.

I enquired why they didn't have baggage and they advised they had only been back from Kosovo two days for a course and were going back to the operation. This was a difficult concept for me to accept, in my mind once you deploy that's it you are there for the duration. I concluded that I had been listening to stories from regular soldiers who had embellished the tales of operations.

So here I was, on an aircraft with two other people. The RAF had loaded the food to the full amount so once were airborne I worked my way through four inflight curries and several deserts.

As we climbed the captain announced we would soon be leaving the UK over Dover. I looked out the window and my home village disappeared underneath me at 12000 feet, you can't help but think will I ever see that again I was off into the unknown.

The crew also pitched in to assist with the inflight meals as they threw away the surplus and it was replenished for the return flight. I sat in the front and chatted to the crew and the other guys. I was called to the cockpit by the captain to see the Alps as we crossed them. What a fantastic sight to observe, the mountains disappearing into the distance with the curvature of the earth clearly visible.

With my imagination racing I wondered how the landing would be, but I remembered this was a civil charter aircraft so the airport must be safe and secure, visions of donning helmets just before touchdown melted away and I enjoyed the descent. We had been in the air for just about an hour and threequarters which passed in no time.

It was early September and a warm wind hit me as I walked out of the aircraft, although it was drizzling it seems just like arriving at a holiday destination in the Mediterranean, the only difference was the occasional person in uniform. The bulk of the ground crew were civilians. As we walked to arrivals, I could see a plethora of different uniforms inside seemingly milling about.

A desk with some RAF personnel was in the middle so I headed for it with my two new friends. This was known as the Airhead where all personnel entered and exited the operational area.

I had my ID card swiped and answered a few questions and I then went to the conveyer to collect the only set of kit and exited the building. Looking around I could have been anywhere in Italy, the scenery in the distance was exactly in the same style as we have found on holiday.

Just outside the door there was a guy wearing a PWRR beret and he asked if I was Major Bennett to which I answered yes with some relief as I had visions of arriving with no one to meet me. We had to go the brigade area first to book in with the quartermaster before going to the police station in Pristina where Bn HQ and B Company were based.

This was to be my home for my time here. On arrival I was delivered to the Quartermaster who said I had arrived just in time for lunch. Another myth busted, I always thought that you ate compo/field rations when operations, how wrong was I, steak chips and mushrooms presented restaurant style, wow I am going to enjoy this I thought! I had met Kevin McCreadie, the QM some years earlier when he was a PSI with 6/7 Queens so it wasn't an awkward meeting.

Kev briefed me over lunch as what would happen next and I felt completely at ease after that. Kevin gave me a new style fleece they were just getting and a new pair of boots that weighed less than my trainers. My opinion of the supply system went up, at least operational troops were getting the best kit at last. I was then sent on a 30-minute drive down into the city and drove into the rear entrance of the police station.

I noted on route many buildings that had been blown out. I found out subsequently these were barracks and government buildings from the old regime which had been taken out with laser guided bunker busting bombs during the airstrikes.

I was taken to the accommodation and dropped all my kit and went to the orderly room to book in. The adjutant, Andy Flay met me and after a situation briefing, we toured the police station and met the key people on site. The Kosovo police service, local police, NATO police and the military police all shared the building, together with B Company 1 PWRR and BHQ meant every piece and useable space was utilised, even the attic was jammed with beds.

I went to the ops room where I would be working and arranged to shadow one of the team after evening meal for six hours. After that I would be working from 16:00 to 23:00 every day. Andy told me he wanted me to take part in all aspects of the operation so I could report back on all aspect of the day to day running of a deployment.

I met the CO and the other officers in station at the evening meal, Col James Cameron was very welcoming towards me, I was the first TA Major they had encountered, rather than being wary everyone without exception was fantastic. I shadowed the ops officer that evening and learned how to deal with weapon finds, shootings and RPG attacks after dark.

I went to bed to reflect on my exciting day. I was just climbing into my sleeping bag and there was a single shot and before I could react a bullet came through the blackout window board and sent up into the roof just above my head. I was out of bed and into my tracksuit like a shot.

I went downstairs and it became obvious what had happened. A platoon was on exchange from the French army and after a patrol, had unloaded their weapons in the unloading bay directly under my window. One private had not done his drills correctly and when he completed the sequence, he still had a round chambered. When he pulled the trigger, the weapon discharged and I received my shock!

The background which led to the conflict in Kosovo goes back to 1389 when the growing Ottoman empire that had its roots with the Moors in Turkey spread up through the Balkan region to land grab and impose their will. Until this happened the area was predominately Christian due to the crusades back in the 11th century.

The Balkans was on the direct overland route to the Holy land and the population rebelled and sadly were confined to small enclaves spread widely across the whole area. This cause mini conflicts through the centuries until the 1918 revolution in Russia.

The leaders of the countries in the Balkans saw that communism would work in their own countries so it was adopted and links were forged with the Russian empire accordingly.

Eventually the whole area would be unified and became Yugoslavia. At the end of WW2 President Tito strengthened the bond with the Soviet Union as the country became occupied on the cessation of hostilities.

The status quo was observed between the Muslims and the Christians during this time but everything came to a head in 1989 when the Berlin wall came down. Without the communist pressures the country became autonomous and then the rival factions across the religious divide wanted more say in how their countries were being run. In 1991 this led to wars between the Muslims and Christians in Croatia, Serbia, Bosnia, Macedonia and then Kosovo in 1999.

The multinational force led by Brigadier Mike Jackson entered Kosovo in the summer of 1999 as a show of force to convince the warring factions to cease hostilities. Eventually this force was to become KFOR and ultimately form the three brigades (North Centre and South) which oversaw the weapon handovers and territory agreements which took some four years to stabilise.

When I was there in 2002 the country was in a nervous peace which enabled another element to come into play. The Mafia presence is strong in Kosovo with people smuggling, drugs and underage workers being shipped all around Europe and beyond. The mafia had no allegiances with either side so in effect they were another element in the multicultural mix that was the Balkans.

After a few days in theatre, I was asked to attend a briefing and lunch at Camp Bondsteel, the headquarters of KFOR and home to the American battalion under command. The CO, adjutant and B Coy commander and I arrived an hour early and went to security to book in. This is where one of the most bizarre things happened. The guard room was just off the main road and the camp was built from scratch on the top of a hill surrounded by rolling countryside.

Some days the sentries used additional security to check our weapons. We had to unload them and with the rifles hold the working parts to the rear and they would drop a ball bearing down the barrel and catch it when it fell out. They then knew the weapon was unloaded. They used a different system to check a pistol.

They used a piece of wire to push down the barrel. Now the piece of wire they were using was so bent and distorted, try as the guy could he couldn't get the wire down the barrel. The CO started to spit feathers when the guard said unless he could get the wire down the barrel I couldn't come in!!

I suggested I dismantled it and give him the barrel which I did but instead of just looking down the barrel he was still trying to push the wire inside. I said to the guy give me the barrel and when he did, I held it up to my eye and said can you see my eye through it and he conceded that it was ok. thirty minutes wasted!

We just made the start of the briefing and the CO and adjutant sat at the front with the brigade hierarchy and I stayed at the back. The briefing lasted approximately thirty minutes and we dispersed for lunch. The CO and Adjutant joined us and we were about to leave when the Brigade commander came by. He saw me and stopped in his tracks. He came over and shook my hand vigorously and said hello John, how are you?

My group just stood there with their mouths open. General Marcel Valentin of course knew me from the exercise in France two years earlier so he invited me to join him for lunch. On our way back to camp I was quizzed over my knowledge of him and how he operated etc. After that encounter the CO always took me on significant visits, even arranging a helicopter to take me back to Pristina in time for my shift in the Ops room.

Even on operations life goes on. The battalion needed to train junior leaders and rather than sending them to Brecon for the normal promotion course they put together a junior nco course based at battalion headquarters under the watchful eye of a couple of the instructors from Brecon.

I was invited to attend the passing out parade, was sat in the front row right next to the CO as the 20 soldiers proudly paraded before us, this was a most surreal experience. The civvie from Canterbury acting as Bn second in command assisting the CO hand out stripes! I was of course rumbled, one of the guys who had earnt his stripe was a guy named Matt Jenkinson whom I knew as a cadet some years ago and the son of a garage owner from Dover that I had been dealing with for years.

He looked me squarely in the eyes and said what the hell are you doing here? I can't wait to tell my dad! We had a laugh and I congratulated him and moved on to the next guy.

I was given a task a couple of days later; I was to take a section and secure the football stadium. The former Governor of Hong Kong, Lord Chris Patten was visiting the central government locally and my job was to provide protection for him once the government security had delivered him to the stadium.

From here he was to fly by helicopter back to the airport for his return to the UK. After he relinquished his governorship, he had taken a job as an EU representative and was working with the fledgling governments in the Balkans to assist in the return to democracy.

We arrived on time and secured the stadium. The helicopter arrived and I went on board to meet the crew. The aircraft was a Russian HIP that had obviously seen some service. The green paint was still clearly visible under the white UN paint with traces of desert camouflage. The body panels had gaps where you could put your finger, the side door wouldn't shut properly and all the seat belts had not been working for years.

The pilot was a big Ukrainian with a huge moustache, in a crisply starched shirt smoking a huge roll up cigarette which did look a little dubious.

Chris Patten arrived late so I knew I couldn't persuade him to go to the airport by road so into the helicopter we went. This was the worst flight I had ever taken.

The airport was only a few minutes away but it seemed like a lifetime. The wind whipped through the gaps in the fuselage, the vibration was horrendous and the noise of the engines roared and clattered through the whole aircraft. Chris Patten has a natural fair complexion but after a few moments he was positively white and bitterly regretting not going by road.

On arrival we bade a quick farewell and off he went into the departure lounge. I decided not to go back to the stadium but to cadge a lift with the R&R transport which by sheer luck was just collecting a few guys. On my return the Ops officer said that didn't look too well and I recounted the mornings events! Mental note to oneself, don't fly in Russian helicopters again!

We had a surplus of vehicles, not many green ones but white painted displaying the UN logo. They were mainly double cab land rovers or Toyota pickup's, there was never a problem booking a vehicle, we had so many of them lined up in the yard. The green fleet was controlled in the usual way but the NATO fleet was very haphazard.

The work in the ops room was either boring or extremely exciting. Some days we would sit through a whole shift without the telephone ringing or the radio bursting into life or I would walk in to a handover and all hell would be breaking loose with multiple events happening within our area of operations.

The first thing I noticed which added to the chaos was the system used to mark incidents on the map. The pins were too confusing when close together and made it difficult to brief the CO or the Ops officer. I had used a different system and after a couple of days implemented it to make life a little easier for the watchkeepers.

It was tradition to put a brief description on a pin on the map but this was always too small to read properly. My system was a series of numbered self-adhesive arrows which related to a sheet with a corresponding number. This enabled a fuller description to be noted down and easier to manage the incidents. This system proved popular and I still believe they use it in the ops room to this day.

Being a bit of a military historian, I knew the value of the war diaries and every shift we had to complete these fully. They were in triplicate with one copy sent to the MOD, the second kept in the battalion and the third one went to the MOD archive. The humbling thought was that incidents that I had managed in 2002 would not see the light of day until they were released in 2042, forty years after I had written them.

I managed many incidents during my time in Pristina, notably weapons finds. For several weeks the local police would walk through the adjoining door advising that a pile of weapons and ammunition had been found stacked on a pavement in a suburb in the North of the City.

I would have to deploy a four-man team to secure the area and make sure it was just a weapon dump not an improvised bomb and then call in other specialists, either bomb disposal or the weapons specialists who deal with the obscure or elderly guns or rocket launchers. The specialists were a brigade asset and not necessarily from the British battalion so there would be a delay if they had to travel from adjacent battalions.

At night there would only be one team of each available, if they were already tasked, we then had to wait until they arrived, not too much of an issue for me but for the guys on the ground it was miserable and cold, but we had no choice.

Perhaps after six hours we could close the incident down and remove it from the ops room board and the quick response guys could go back to bed. Quite often this would happen nightly and in the same place. It transpired that the local Muslim militia had an excess of hardware and had a deep-rooted suspicion in the authorities hence the sneaky way they got rid of the goodies.

We did spread the word that it would be no problem simply to turn up with a truck full and no questions asked but I suppose the whole region had gone through incredible change through the past decade that trust was hard to cement. So, there we were every night for a week clearing weapons, some of which pre-dated WW1.

One night the adjoining door burst open and a policeman from the NATO team came bursting into the ops room. An RPG had been fired through the front window of a pharmacy and blown the whole shop front out. This event took all evening to sort out with all three police forces, the brigade QRF and elements of our B Coy the telephones and radios did not stop and my head was spinning when I went to bed that evening.

A strange phenomenon occurred during September every year. Autumn in the Balkan region was usually very pleasant enabling everyone to walk around outside in shirt sleeves, but on the eleventh of the month winter starts. I went to bed on the evening of the tenth at around eighteen degrees and woke up at one degree with an inch of snow on the ground.

What a bizarre experience, I was told that this event was so accurate you could set your watch by it. Suddenly fleeces, Norwegians and smocks were the norm.

A few days before I went for a walk in the city with Andy Smith the B Coy commander, we went up the hill to the Pristina Memorial to the fallen partisans in WW2. This was situated on a hillside overlooking the city and very striking in its design and quite thought provoking. Andy explained the tactical situation which had led up to the start in the conflict as we walked around the city and it certainly was food for thought. How the population had suffered so many wars within living memory was so incredible and so hard to come to terms with.

When we were in the police station, we didn't carry our weapons around with us, they stayed in the armoury. As the battalion was augmented by watchkeepers, additional specialists etc there was a need to have pool weapons.

I was allocated a browning 9mm pistol, very similar to the one I owned and used at the local pistol club. Mine own weapon was tight on the slide and wouldn't move if you tried to twist the slide sideways, but the one I was issued was all floppy and looked as if it had been fired far too many times.

I also suspect it would have would have failed its annual REME inspection. I hoped that I would never have to put this to the test, but events panned out differently a little later.

One of the very sad things that came out of the war was that so many families were displaced quickly, to avoid the killings and religion-based murders that happened prior to NATO involvements. In most cases families left their homes in the clothes they were standing up in, leaving behind their possessions and their pets.

This resulted in the ten years that followed significant in breeding occurred, and there were over one million stray dogs roaming around. They tended to populate the cities as food in dustbins was easier to come by. These animals were mostly rabid and covered in sores and wounds, which made them look very sad.

The government wanted to encourage people to move back to the cities but these viscous and nasty animals were a blocker to many people. It was decided to have a major cull and the Swedish battalion had trained hunters, who had shotguns and were well versed in this type of activity.

We had to provide security for this task and I decided to go with one of the patrols to observe events as they unfolded. The cull was done just after dawn before the animals awoke, they were in packs and many animals lived in these groups so they were easier to deal with.

We met up with the Swedes and walked around the suburbs for about fifteen minutes, until we came across a group of sleeping dogs under a half destroyed shed. The guys took aim and killed several dogs with their pump action shotguns.

One animal though was a cross bull mastiff, ugly, huge and covered and sores and an ear missing. It didn't take kindly to being shot at and was up in a flash and charging straight towards me. I was about thirty meters away watching the road, assisting with the security and didn't see the wounded animal approaching.

One of the guys shouted a warning and I took to my heels. The Swedes couldn't get a clear shot as I was too close, the brute was closing on me even though it was limping. I was very concerned when I could hear its breathing and there was nowhere high to go. In the end I drew my pistol and had to shoot it in the head. It dropped a foot away from me.

Absolute relief and I decided to return early to the police station for a sit down with a coffee. Bizarre things operations, they give you weapons to protect yourselves but when you use them you have to fill out many sheets of paper. Shooting a dog was not in the approved list so many questions were asked.

Eventually I went back to my bunk via the B Coy CQMS to collect one new replacement round which I signed for. Somehow at the end of the tour I was deemed to be one round missing and had to complete more paperwork. I was going to be a little more selective on what I got involved in going forward!

The next day I decided to go on a foot patrol into the city centre. We were dropped off at the partly finished cathedral that the Christians were building prior to the fall of communism.

Although it was just a shell it was deemed as a target for Muslim extremists as it was a symbol of Christianity. We had to guard this 24/7 to avoid issues. We patrolled past the library, this looked very futuristic in its appearance, and was untouched by any of the troubles. We meandered down through the city until we came across a small square surrounded by cafés.

As we rounded the corner a burst of gunfire echoed. There was a guy laying on the ground bleeding and a guy standing over him with an AK47. We walked cautiously forward and when the gunman saw us, he stopped moving and looked very sheepish. It was obvious he had no intent so we walked up and I disarmed him. The guys plasticuffed him and we secured the area until the police arrived. More paperwork!

The rest of the day was spent in the police area being interviewed and drinking endless tea. It transpired that it was a mafia related shooting and not within our jurisdiction so the police took it forward from there and we heard no more. Another interesting day in the office, I was beginning to think that operational experience was paperwork heavy!

The de-escalation of belligerence between the Christians and the Muslims allowed us to send most of the battalions AFV Warrior's back to Tidworth. We also didn't wear our helmets when we were out on the streets to show a softer side to the population and an aura of confidence that their world was gradually returning to normal. B Coy were to do a patrol up towards one of our bases in the North and I agreed to command it. I had never seen a warrior up close before, and being a commander of four of them was quite something. It was an uneventful patrol and it turned out to be the last one before the warriors were sent back to the UK.

I attached myself to civpop liaison and visited some of the more affected communities. Life was returning to normal but kept up a presence in the outlying areas. The Christian minority were pleased with these visits and showed extreme hospitality to us and celebrated our visit with slivovitz which is a high-octane spirit made from plums which grow prolifically in the Balkan region.

This stuff was evil rather similar to Vodka and drunk straight down in one! You had to toast everyone and everything, after one visit I went back to Pristina and went to bed for a few hours, awaking five minutes before my shift started.

Thankfully it was a quiet night and I gave myself a day off the next day. Plums really don't agree with my digestion and I usually steer clear of them but the slivovitz worked its magic. The following evening the ops room was devoid of the senior watch keeper for long spells during the evening, whilst the plums exacted their revenge!

One evening one of the NATO police officers came in and we had a brew. I was fascinated how UK police officers were working with NATO. This particular officer, again his name escapes me was a serving officer from the Norfolk constabulary on a two-year attachment together with seven other officers, worked with the local police teaching and mentoring processes.

They all lived in a large house in the suburbs in a quiet area. What struck me was this guy was in his early 50s obviously a career officer but had felt the need to work in a different environment. He had done weapon training as they all had hand guns and were held in high esteem by all the enforcement authorities.

For a time, their boss was the former head of the Northern Ireland police service, Ronnie Flanagan who I worked with during an operation as his ADC. I admired these guys; they didn't have to be there but they helped develop a basis for law enforcement.

They didn't get salary enhancements to do this important task which amazed me. They did get food and accommodation for free but they worked way over their normal shift hours, sometimes in extreme danger. I have only the utmost respect for these guys, they didn't need to be there but as always with the police they are fearless and implement the rule of law 100% without fear or concern.

The day of my return loomed and on the morning of my departure saw me at breakfast on my own, something was going down up north and the whole company had deployed together with the headquarters elements.

I went to the ops room to say good bye and the only guy on duty was Si Hewer who was our signals psi in the previous months in Canterbury. We said our goodbyes and I left to return to the UK.

It felt strange to go, just to leave it was quite surreal. I went through departures and swiped my ID card and I was off. A full aircraft this time and before I knew it, I was standing outside the arrival's hall looking for my driver. When I enquired at the information desk, I was advised I had another one way hire to drive home. Again, no bells whistles or flags, off went Bennett into the night.

Arriving home was an anti-climax, after a good night sleep I was back to work as if nothing had happened. It was a most surreal experience, two days earlier I had been doing close protection to visiting generals, hand hovering on my pistol, radio in hand and then I was looking at a damaged front wing on a ford escort van.

Nothing seemed real or mattered the feeling of operations puts you in a bubble. Your senses are heightened. I tried to explain to my boss how it felt, but all he was interested in was productivity and customer service, he didn't have a clue!
For a few weeks I was looking over my shoulder jumping at the slightest bang, or ducking at the slightest unusual sound.

This is quite common for everyone returning back from ops but the regulars have what is known as decompression. They go somewhere for a bit of R&R on route home, this could include a trip to a training camp on Salisbury plain or the ski lodges in the Bavarian mountains etc, just for a few days to unwind in a safe place as companies or platoons, before going home to their families.

This continued for a week or so back at the battalion then after 2 weeks leave all went back to normal. I suppose these days, I would have experienced what is now known as an adjustment disorder, quite common for those who work through high intensity stress, and then suddenly return back to their normal environment. There is an effective treatment these days but back then, I had to work through it on my own.

I was invited back to the battalion about a month later to meet HM the Queen of Denmark when she visited the battalion. A huge party was organised and HM met the families and the guys and watched demonstrations and events put on for the visit. All this was done in a huge field on the plain and on a superb late summers' day.

HM was fascinated to hear of my exploits and we all enjoyed a magnificent lunch and it was good to catch up with the guys I had worked with in Pristina. I kept in touch with the battalion for a couple of years and met up with the officers at the annual officer's club dinner at the end of November.

I lost touch with most of the guys when they deployed to Iraq where they became the most decorated infantry battalion since WW2 with one VC and innumerable high-level awards following the battle of Danny Boy and the siege of CIMIC house where the guys acquitted themselves incredibly well.

It was hard to take in that less than eighteen months earlier I was introduced over breakfast to the CO designate Lt Col Matt Maer who would lead the battalion during this operation and receive a CBE for his outstanding leadership.

When I attended the next training evening, I was debriefed by the CO who advised me that I was to plan and put into practise the type of operational training I had been doing. This was known as peace support operations. To be fair I think they had been waiting for me to return for this very reason as they had a gap in the training plan.

The brigade was very helpful in supplying unusual weapons and blanks for them together with a supply of loan pistols. We were able to run a battalion exercise at Imber village on Salisbury plain based on my planning which gave me huge satisfaction. I was quite confident the battalion could undertake this type of operation without too much training.

Our battalion second in command was unable to attend training and I was asked to stand in for him as well as organise the battalions training schedule and run a company! A very busy time laid ahead! I wrote my report for Chilwell and following this some of my recommendations for returning attached personnel were implemented regarding the decompression process.

We began to work with the civil authorities far more than ever before around this time. Lessons were learned from the Foot and Mouth crisis and it became obvious that the military needed to an integral part of any disaster whether a weather catastrophe or a terrorism incident.

We did many exercises with the authorities, our unit was the lead military unit in our brigade area, we produced a modified command post tent out of a 12x12 tent with flaps to take a 9x9.

We had the ability to put together a command cell in the field using five vehicles attached to the larger tent. This cell would contain the Engineers, medical, transport and the infantry unit command teams with the central area for briefings.

In my final year of service, we were told our unit had been selected to attend an oversees exercise in none other than Kazakhstan. The crusty Cold war warriors amongst us were quite excited to hear this, as finally after so many years we would see the old soviet kit up close.

We were to be field firing range packages and training with the local Kazaks. This would culminate with a joint exercise and a day off in Almaty the largest city in the country which until recently had been the capital.

The logistics of getting us here dictated how many of the guys could actually attend this unique exercise. We could only take the equivalent of two VC10s capacity plus the Q party in the Hercules that transported the infrastructure and the ammunition. We were to refuel at Cyprus as part of the ten-hour flight.

I was initially unsure if I would be going, we needed range qualified staff plus enough officers to attend the events planned for us as hosts. There also needed to have enough troops to actually do the training and the various formal parades that we knew would happen over the two weeks we were there.

Eventually I was selected to be part of the CO's team and to run the grouping and zeroing range. The day dawned and we donned our desert kit and floppy hats and off to RAF Brize Norton. There sat an aging VC10 with the previous one having departed four hours earlier due to air traffic control issues.

Brize was a place I knew quite well having been there a few times over the years. The place hadn't changed much since my Kosovo deployment other than it now needed a lick of paint. I can imagine how many soldiers had passed through here since I was here last, but it certainly needed a refurbish!

We boarded the aircraft and I had forgotten the seats were rearwards facing. This takes a bit of getting used to and once airborne we thought nothing of it. Cyprus was a four-hour flight and only when we were on the ground did, we find out a very worrying fact. The aircraft had two fuel tanks but one of them couldn't be used due to a problem with getting the parts.

We had to leave the aircraft whilst it was refuelled so we went to the departure lounge and took advantage of the air conditioning. The temperature in Cyprus in early August was forty degrees plus so no sitting outside in the sun for us!

When we returned to our seats and started to taxi out to the runway, I noticed an SR71 Blackbird sitting between two hangers, so clearly the Americans were using our airfield for their observations on Saddam Hussein's Iraq. You don't see these every day so definitely a tick in the box!

We took off and headed to Kazakhstan, after a while I went up to the flight deck to chat to the pilots, they were a little busy playing cards and the aircraft was on autopilot. The pilots also didn't seem any older than their early twenties - how old did I feel!

The view in the cockpit was amazing, flying at over thirty-nine thousand feet the earths curvature clearly visible and the mountains far below covered in snow looked amazing. We had a few hours on this leg so I unrolled my sleeping bag and had a sleep on the floor.

The first day in camp was a little chaotic, the range teams were sent out to the Steppe and to work out where we could set up a challenging field firing range. Basically, we had two hundred miles of rolling countryside where the only green thing growing were cannabis plants, we just set up and marked the extreme left and right boundaries and that was it.

We returned to camp and queued for supper. As always, the officers ate last and as we approached the front of the queue, we realised by the mutterings that the food had run out. Most of the senior nco' s had not eaten in front of us and they were giving the chef hell. A simple miscalculation had resulted in fifty hungry officers and nco' s, the senior chef was tired after the long journey in the Hercules and we paid the price.

After a day with temperatures in the 40's and no food at the end of it meant some really grumpy people were going to bed grumbling. I shared my packet of biscuits with the five other guys in my tent. Breakfast and onwards was fine and back on track but a very sheepish chef kept his head down!

My task was to run the grouping and zeroing range and then act as safety supervisor when the range package started. All the weapons had been brought over in bundles and this always put them out of zero so A full G&Z had to be completed before you could move to the field firing phase.

I set up my range and awaited the first detail. The range was a fixed range with the ability to engage targets from twenty-five metres out to two hundred metres but we would only be using the nearest ones. The firing point had a metal frame and a tin roof with a low frame about eighteen inches off the ground.

There was a separate structure on each firing point. We worked our details and had nearly completed the task when the guy to my right started to wave his weapon around and then he turned pointing his weapon to the guy on his left. I leapt across to grab him but forgot the frame at shin height.

I toppled forward and fell onto the guy and he dropped his weapon, instinct had stopped an incident but crikey did my leg hurt. I hobbled over to see the medics and the doctor said I had damaged the tissue and the membrane on the bone on the shin. I spent the rest of the day in the med tent with ice on my leg.

The swelling meant I could not wear my boots so it precluded me working on the field firing ranges. I really felt for the safety teams, they worked all day in the blistering heat. The camp water was kept in the chiller but on the ranges, it was just hot in the bottle and quite unpalatable. For the remainder of the camp and indeed for the next four months I couldn't wear my boots, trainers just didn't look the same with uniform.

The camp where we stayed was just a grassy area to the rear of a large complex of ranges within view of the snow-capped mountains which constituted the Chinese border. When I say grass, I really mean dust with a few small cannabis plants dotted about. The camp was completed tented, with a large communal mess tent adjacent to some really unusual cooking equipment. To the rear of the cooking area there was a shipping container fitted out as a chiller to store all the perishable food.

As a Cold war warrior there was a real treat for me. Adjacent to the tented camp there was a decommissioned cold war bunker with missile silos and ops room. We were invited to visit the ops room, so at the appointed time we headed off to a set of steps which led to a huge set of doors, beyond this the stairs disappeared downwards. The tiled walls wouldn't have looked out of place in a London underground station, quite light and bright.

There was a very long corridor which opened up into a large room with smaller rooms leading from it. The large room was still fitted out with all the cold war equipment even the maps on the wall still showed the targets on the west coast of the USA.

We had a briefing and a bit of history which was fascinating about the command centre which culminated in an invite to lunch. This was our first exposure to a traditional business lunch in the region.

On arrival we saw a huge table of food with many well-presented staff waiting on hand. The Kazaks were waiting and the drinks reception started. There was a huge choice of 'refreshments' waiting and the traditional toasts started. Vodka was served in large glasses and in the traditional way of the Kazaks, we had to toast and drink straight down which is fine but the strength of the vodka was off the scale and it dawned on me that first was the first of many toasts.

We toasted the President, our Queen and Prime Minister, and after a blur in time I think we even toasted my cat! Lunch was eventually served in a haze and it was only a little later I realised there was some orange juice available so that was the last time I did the heavy stuff.

There were more of these lunches over the next week, the battalion command group and those not on the ranges had to attend and some pretty sore heads were evident, all for the international relations.

In the second week we had a reception at the UK's ambassador's residence in Almaty which was pleasant with canapes and wine and beer. Not a vodka in sight which pleased the CO and the battalion second in command as they had suffered a bit over a few recent lunch times. When this concluded we moved on to a restaurant for supper, donning traditional robes and hats for the occasion. After its conclusion we had a long ride home and prepared for the exercise over the next day or so.

We participated in a friendship parade in the centre of Almaty near the impressive memorial to the fallen in WW2 with our hosts. Great pomp and tradition shown by all during this event.

A huge event was also organised in camp for us where various Kazak special forces, marines and a plethora of other services put on displays of tactics and weapon handling. This was followed by speeches and awards and certificates, all done under the watchful generals, politicians and the press. Clearly this was all stage managed for the wider audience.

The tents were hot at night and the toilet facilities were a little pungent, my old friend the turdis was present and it became a little unhealthy towards the end of the exercise. The showers were rudimentary, little more than a shed with a huge water tank topped up every day by a tanker. If you had a shower in the morning it was cold and in the evening after a blistering day in the sun, boiling hot so timing was essential.

The CO's command group got on with preparing for the exercise which compared to the exercises in recent years, was quite significant. The exercise was held on the ranges which were unlike anything in the UK, they were longer that four kilometres width wise and seemed to go to infinity into the distance.

They were able to use artillery and mortars so the firing points were not what we were used to. The Kazaks threw everything at this exercise, they arranged a paratroop drop BRDM-2 wheeled personal carriers, tanks and other armour. A team of special forces worked with us together with their regular troops.

The exercise culminated with all participants doing a drive by to the hierarchy on the viewing platform overlooking the ranges, who duly took the salute. The guys were in BRDM-2 armoured wheeled personnel carriers.

As an observer, I couldn't help feeling that the structure and the conduct of the exercise was engineered to please the

Generals and the press corps on the viewing tower, not actually displaying any training value.

During some down time when I couldn't go out of camp, I had the opportunity to view a display of old cold war vehicles which were still in use with the Kazak army. This helped to put the threat all those years ago into perspective.

We were always told the might of the Soviets was all powerful and we should rightly fear them. Having crawled all over them I was not so sure of their capability to rule the world.

The ZSU57 self-propelled anti-aircraft gun for instance seemed to be very poorly built with panels out of line before being welded with thin steel plate etc.

The dreaded T72 tank which we had feared coming across the horizon back in the day wasn't quite as fearless close up. The crew compartment was incredibly cramped. All the crew needed to be no taller than five feet high and extremely underweight to spend any time inside.

How these crews could work in this environment for weeks on end amazed me. I couldn't even fit in the commander's position, my body protruded from the waist upwards and no matter how I wriggled and twisted I could get low enough to get the hatch shut. I suppose the build weaknesses were made up by the sheer volume available to the tank battalions. We did look round a T62 which seemed a sturdier vehicle, the drive rollers, track structure and armour seemed a much higher quality than its successor.

In 1989 the world events contributed to the downfall of the Soviet Union. All the individual countries within the union went back to self-rule. The equipment and units sitting in the individual countries became their own forces and their nationals were transferred back to their own countries.

This of course had its advantages and disadvantages; the units may have been low grade and poorly equipped and conversely have been top line. I suspect that Moscow would have drawn these back under their control before the agreed transfer date.

The T72 we looked did not appear to be in good condition, the tracks and rollers were very worn and it looked very much as if it would break down at the earliest opportunity. Because the T62 and T72 were on display I assumed that this was all the Kazaks had in terms of armour, there was no sign of a T80 which was a completely different and an advanced piece of equipment.

At the end of camp, we returned home but we didn't have the Hercules to transport the excess kit and ammunition. The weapons were put in bundles in the hold of the VC 10. They had quite a substantial amount of ammunition left over, but was all of different calibre to the weapons the Kazaks used. Plus, it would have been questionable if we had simply given it away so the Ammunition Technical officer took it all out to the ranges, together with some antitank rockets and simply blew the whole lot up.

A huge plume of smoke drifted across the ranges and the sound of the bang echoed around the complex for what seemed like minutes.

We were moved back to Almaty airfield and saw in the distance the V shaped tail planes of the two VC10's some distance before our arrival. The airport building looked harsh and basic but we were driven past it and taken to the other end of the airfield and entered through a side gate.

Awaiting us was a group of UK service personnel who had come out on the flight to administer us. There were movements guys from the RLC, two corporals from the RMP, RAF ground crew and a few others.

Once we had got our kit in rows and sorted out which VC10 we would be travelling on, we had a series of briefings and to our amazement we received a stern talking to about the dangers of drugs and that we shouldn't use them or bring them back into the country.

We all fell about laughing and the burly female corporal from the RAF police didn't take too kindly to this at all she had just flown out from Brize Norton on a nine-hour flight to give us this lecture, which it turned out was normal practise for such an exercise no matter where in the world it was. The corporal didn't know that all that was green growing around us was in fact cannabis!

She showed us an MFO box and told us that we could put any drugs inside and no questions would be asked. She was going to disappear for ten minutes. We as soon as she went, the guys ripped up as many cannabis plants as they could and stacked the box to about four feet high with them! When she returned, she went red in the face and shouted that it was no joking matter.

To us of course who had been running around in 40 degrees plus temperatures and tired and drained, thought it was hilarious. We retired under the wings for shade and watched them with interest while they searched the box for anything else. We were issued a cardboard RAF horror box with some very old and curly sandwiches inside and we boarded the aircraft.

The flight home was long and tedious making the same stop in Cyprus utilising the floor space for sleeping once again. The aircraft was cool and it felt so comfortable after the recent heat.

When we unloaded at Brize Norton chaos ensured. We were certain the RAF corporal had radioed ahead because the RMP drugs search dogs were waiting for us. We were tired and grumpy after a long flight, and to be held up in arrivals was more tedious than I can explain. The drugs dogs went mad, they were all over us and our kit to some amusement, because no one had realised we had been walking, running and laying around on and in cannabis plants.

All our clothes were impregnated together with webbing and day sacks and even sleeping bags, you could smell it in the air over there, sometimes it was so pungent it gave you a headache.

After the CO explained to the senior nco of the RMP we boarded the coaches and headed home. A thoroughly good exercise, not many people get to see the Chinese border for free!

Chapter 22

The finale

By early 2005 I had been OC of HQ Coy for five years. I was wanting new challenges but was struggling to find a job that would provide this outside the battalion so I reluctantly decided to hang up my boots.

Having been acting battalion second in command, TA training major, there was nothing more I could achieve in the battalion. Robin MaCalpine - Downey was chomping at my heels to take over the company so I knew the time was right.

I retired on the first of July 2005 the day I qualified for the bar to my VRSM. As if by fate, three days later I was promoted at work and was destined to work away from home for the next seven years, so realistically I would not have had time to devote to the TA to the level I would have wanted to.

About three weeks later I received a call from the commander 2 Bde's PA asking if I could come and have coffee with him. I agreed as I thought he wanted to thank me for my years of service. This he did but also asked if I would reconsider leaving. The powers to be were considering setting up a course at Sandhurst for the guys commissioning as late entry.

There had not been something like this when I commissioned and you had to pretty much learn on the job but a structured onc-week course would be much better for those coming along behind.

It would mean I could start with a clean slate, devise and present the course and choose my own team of instructors. A fantastic opportunity and what an accolade, to choose the content was unheard of.

My work promotion would open doors for me and I knew that I could not sustain the level of intensity the course would need to make it work effectively. Also, the potential for a call up this time to Iraq was looming, I knew I couldn't do this due to family commitments.

A few days later I received a call from Col Richard Dixon, my former CO, now honorary colonel, asking if I would consider being Deputy Commandant of Kent ACF. I seized the opportunity to maintain contact with the military, but working with cadets was a different game altogether.

I attended a board at brigade headquarters and was appointed to the role with promotion to Lt Colonel. There was a certain amount of jealousy from the existing officers in the cadet headquarters, who made it clear that they should have been appointed. I did manage to work with these guys but sadly, even with this low commitment I knew I would not be reliable enough or give the role the intensity it deserved so I resigned my commission after nine months.

I heard around this time that I had been awarded a Commander Land Forces Meritorious Certificate, for which I was extremely proud, after all I was just doing my job.

Over the next couple of years, I missed the TA terribly, it had been a huge part of my life for twenty-seven years and to suddenly stop was a real shock to the system. What did I miss the most? It wasn't the work or the excitement, it was the people.

The guys in my company mostly had come through with me on my journey, some of the senior guys in the Signals platoon were just joining when I was a corporal! So, I had known 80% of the company for well over twenty years!

In addition, the permanent staff were outstanding, some of them had worked there before I joined. My company admin officer, Janet Skates was so efficient and was outstanding, I was lucky to work with her for the five years I commanded HQ company. The staff in battalion HQ who also kept the wheels oiled, Shelley and Lesley worked with Henry Thomas to administer the battalion, through all the challenges the brigade threw at them. I know it's necessary but last-minute statistics needed yesterday always caused implosions but they always came up with the goods.

The REME vehicle mechanic Darryl (Jeff) Key was in the MT platoon before I joined and we were great friends, he had served his apprenticeship with Barrett's of Canterbury in their commercial division before he decided to join up, he was a train driver when I first met him.

When a vacancy in the permanent staff arose for his role came up, he jumped at the chance. We had shared many a cold and wet night over the years and indeed a holiday or two. Sadly, he was killed in an accident a year after I left which devastated his family and all those who knew him.

I think that I took a great deal away from the TA, it gave me free management training, taught me how to be diplomatic, have humility, respect for your seniors and above all respect the soldiers who look up to you for help and guidance. I learnt to type and use computer's, was given every group of driving licence including HAZMAT for free and the most important thing was the friendships made for life.

Not bad for a guy who only attended half of his primary education due to illness and spent the majority of his life playing catch up!

Photographs

Endex Bold Guard 1978. My platoon at the end of the exercise waiting for the transport back to camp. L to R, Paul Barker, Willie Rushton, author, Jim Dew, Mick Page and Private Harrison. Credit John Bennett

Final training weekend before a driving competition. Chris Hulks, Harry Cook with author on the right. Credit John Bennett

Vogelsang. Photograph taken for local paper, no one told the MP what we were doing, he was getting more nervous. His finger kept rubbing the safety catch. Credit Gerry Warren, KM group

Exercise Eternal Triangle, Pete Bartlett (second from the left) just before the smoke started. Note the motorway just above us with the rain obscuring the building behind us in the photo. Credit John Bennett

Measles holes. The demolition charges were suspended from the bar shown. Credit Charlie Simcoe

UBRE at work. Pete Bartlett behind the door. Credit John Bennett

MT platoon taking first aid training seriously. Credit John Bennett

HGV training cadre, Students and instructors. Credit John Bennett

HQ Coy shooting champions 1989. Credit Gerry Warren KM Group

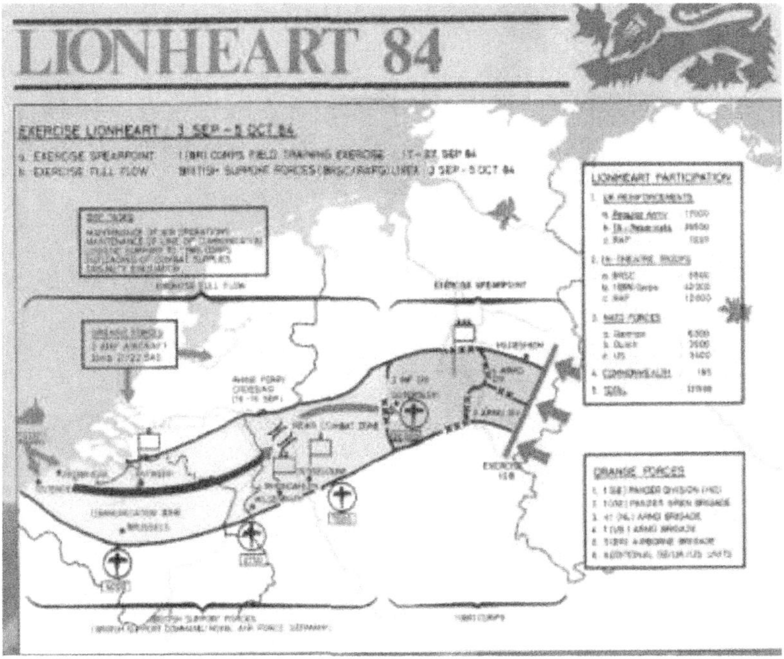

Exercise Lionheart deployment chart. Credit MOD

John Bennett and Rodney Stockford pretending to be important.
Credit Barry Duffield, Media Ops

Author outside MNB (C) Headquarters, Pristina. Credit John Bennett

Bombed out police headquarters with football stadium to the left. Taken from Ops room window in Pristina. Credit John Bennett

Author in 1PWRR operations room in Pristina Credit John Bennett

Julian Ladd and author. Credit John Bennett

The final Warrior patrol. Credit John Bennett

Author, Lt Col Patrick Crowley and RSM(WO1) Julian Whatley. Credit Barry Duffield, Media Ops

A hard day on the ranges in Kazakhstan with Nigel Sutton.
Credit John Bennett

Preparing for G&Z range. Note the cannabis behind author's shoulder! Credit John Bennett

ZSU57 SP anti aircraft gun. Credit John Bennett

Officers mess dinner in traditional Kazak attire. Credit Nigel Sutton

One of the last photos taken before retirement. Very poignant as I am standing on the bridge at Thetford where Jack Bright and myself went fishing with a hand grenade all those years before. Credit John Bennett

The final photograph taken on exercise before retirement at Thetford training area. Credit John Bennett

Handing over the company to Robin MaCalpine Downey in May 2005.
Credit John Bennett

The author being interviewed by the BBC commemorating the 20th anniversary of the death of Diana, Princess of Wales, former Colonel in Chief of the PWRR. Credit BBC television

The author and Lance Sergeant Johnson Beharry VC, taken at Guildford on the 1st July 2016 while commemorating the 100th anniversary of the battle of the Somme. The PWRR and Queen's regiment mobile museum artefacts including the 8th Bn East Surreys football in the glass case. Credit John Bennett

Afterword

'John Bennett paints a colourful and lively picture of being a citizen soldier during the Cold War. His anecdotal style is by turns funny, moving and thoughtful. So many of his stories strike an echo for anyone who served during that period: the deployments to Germany, the cold and wet days on the ranges, the comradeship and the discipline – superficially very like regular service but with that extra bounce you get when the soldiers all have another job and are there because they want to be, at the end of a hard week at their civilian jobs.

John's service with the Queens and latterly the PWRR, as it became, was based at Leros barracks, Canterbury's only link with the Army now the (regular) Howe Barracks has gone. He paints an attractive picture of local men (they were all men in the infantry then, rightly or wrongly) enjoying and – occasionally not enjoying – part-time soldiering. I remember the frustration he describes of having to abandon training because of last minute cuts to budgets,

It is easy to forget now the serious purpose behind all this. Outnumbered by the overwhelming might of the Soviet Bloc the Territorial Army was a vital part of our defences. It had proved its worth in both world wars and, with its new name, The Army Reserve, is needed as much today as at any time since the end of the Cold War. As a former Territorial myself, I recommend this book to anyone who wants to hear about citizen soldiering in the Cold War era and enjoy an easy read.'

Sir Julian Brazier TD

Glossary of terms

AFG1033. Army form for issue and receipt of stores and equipment, a much used and abused form!

ADC. Aide De Camp is an officer who assists a more senior officer acting as a foil and liaison tasks.

Agricola 8. Operation Agricola was the name given to the peace support operation in Kosovo following on from the UN and NATO led move into the country in 1999 to relieve the humanitarian crisis recently identified. Agricola 8 refers to the period of 2001 to 2002 when the 1st Battalion the Princess of Wales's Royal Regiment was deployed on this operation.

AFV. Armoured Fighting Vehicle.

APOD. This refers to the Air Point of Departure. Formerly known as the Airhead.

Armour. Term for tanks and heavy vehicles steered by their tracks.

Armourer. REME technician specialising in weapon repair.

AK47. The most massed produced automatic assault rifle ever made. Designed in 1947 by Alexandrei Kalashnikov it has been sold under licence to China and North Korea. Millions of them have been made at a very small cost. Favoured weapon of terrorists and fanatical groups because of the availability on the world market both of the 7.62 short round it fires and the weapon itself. Oddly it has a single shot facility in which mode it is a very accurate weapon, but thankfully all the owners of these use it in fully automatic when its accuracy becomes thankfully questionable?

BRDM 2. BRDM is an initialism for Boyevaya Razvedyvatelnaya Dozornaya Mashina literally 'Combat Reconnaissance Patrol Vehicle'. The BRDM is a four-wheeled amphibious vehicle which is very lightly armoured by today's

standards. Both versions were produced in the Soviet Union and other Eastern Bloc countries.
Battlegroup. A Battlegroup is an Infantry battalion, plus or minus additional companies. Embedded in this group is usually a squadron of tanks, engineer support and an artillery battery. This provides all the necessary firepower and support for mounting effective operations. A battlegroup trainer brings together all these elements to work through desktop exercises without the troops.
Benghazi Burner. Invented by the British army in the desert in 1942. Consisted of a 40-gallon oil drum with airholes in the sides and filled up to half way with sand. A gallon of petrol poured into one of the these would burn well for a couple of hours to keep soldiers warm at night. If no oil drum was available then petrol poured into sand worked nearly as well!
Bier Keller. A large bar mainly serving beer. These are associated with Bavaria. They have the appearance of a large spacious barn with long wooden tables and trestle seating.
Blinds. This is the term for a piece of ordnance that didn't explode when it should have done.
Blocking Force. This is a combination of infantry and armour placed to deny an enemy a route to either stop them or force them to change direction enabling a greater force to engage them.
Buffs Sunday. The name given locally to the annual reunion and Cathedral parade of the Queens Own Buffs regimental association held in Canterbury on the 1st Sunday in August every year.
BAOR. British Army of the Rhine. Came into being after the standing forces of occupation in 1947 became a force monitoring the regeneration of the West German nation.
Bratwurst mit Frites unt Mayonnaise. German sausage with chips and mayonnaise. Staple diet of military drivers.

CO. Commanding Officer. Officer in charge of a Battalion size unit, usually a Lieutenant Colonel.
CGS. Chief of the General staff. Senior military person based in MOD Whitehall.
Chipmunk. 2-seater RAF trainer aircraft through the 1960s and 1970s. Replaced in early 1980s by the Bulldog.
Currywurst. German sausage usually bratwurst with a curry sauce made from tomato ketchup and mild curry powder mixed cold.
Comms. Comms is a shortened version of communications or to communicate.
Cap comforter. A predominately woollen piece of clothing in the shape of a tube. Today you would refer to one as a snood. They were either worn over the head tucked into the top of your jumper and covered your lower face or fashioned into a hat similar to the style worn by WW2 commando's.
CIMIC House. CIMIC-House was the British Army-led Multi-National Division (South-East)'s centre of Civil-Military Co-operation activities in the Iraqi town of Al Amarah. It was situated in the former residence of the Ba'ath Party governor of Maysan province.
COMKFOR. Commander, Kosovo Force.
CNN. Cable News Network, a US 24hrs news channel.
Danny Boy. The Battle of Danny Boy took place close to the city of Al Amarah in Southern Iraq on 14 May 2004, between British soldiers and about 100 Iraqi insurgents of the Mahdi Army. The battle is named after a local British checkpoint called Danny Boy.
DN3270. A very small digger steered by its tracks.
DS. Directing Staff, these can be specific officers or senior NCO's who are running or umpiring a whole exercise or a phase within a major exercise.
Dr Beeching. Dr Richard Beeching, was a physicist and engineer who for a short but very notable time was chairman of British

Railways and an affiliate of the Labour Party in Britain who developed a plan to save a significant amount of money by closing a large amount of rural railway lines.
EU Regulations. These were a set of rules imposed on all European countries in the 1980 through the 1990 to standardise all rules regarding working hours and use of vehicles. They were designed to allow the free movement of people, vehicles and systems without border controls and having to fill in paperwork at each country. Good in principle but became very bureaucratic as it developed.
Echelon. These are the collective name for groupings of vehicles with various combat supplies and manpower. The 1st line stores and combat supplies (enough for 24 hours) are kept on vehicles broken down into company packets at A1 echelon. A typical A1 Echelon would be commanded by the MTO and would consist of the command post, company CQMS groups. A REME fitter, HQ company storemen. Medics, Support weapons CQMS i.e., MILAN, Mortar and Machine Gun platoon. The Signals platoon would also have a representative as he charged the radio batteries for the rifle company platoons. This would be located very close to the forward companies for ease of resupply. The A2 Echelon would normally have all the battalion troop carrying vehicles, three days combat supplies, mainly ground dumped, REME repair shop, Regimental Aid Post, HQ Coy CQMS to administer the echelon, The UBRE, ground dumped fuel, elements of the clerical team, chefs, armourers, and storemen. This would be commanded by OC HQ Coy as the BLO (Battalion Logistics Officer). This would be located approximately six to ten km behind the A1 Echelon. Finally, the B Echelon would be located within the Brigade admin area for ease of collecting stores and equipment. This was commanded by the Quartermaster and consisted of his team, orderly room and soldiers backloaded for

light duties. The BCR's (Battle Casualty Replacements) were held here prior to moving forward to the rifle companies.
Elze Small town built around a railhead, nine miles south east of Hildesheim in lower Saxony to the rear of the Sibbesse gap. Usually this is where our A2 echelon would be located.
Esbjerg. Port on North Sea coast in Denmark.
G&Z Grouping and zeroing refers to the aligning of a weapon to a user so both can hit a target accurately.
GDP. Gross Domestic Product value of the earnings of UK industry.
General Purpose Machine Gun. Known as a GPMG (referred to as a GIMPY with the G pronounced as a J) This weapon took over as the infantry section heavy hit weapon from the old Lee Enfield Bren gun. It was a modified FN weapon firing 7.62 rounds which came in 200 round links. A very effective weapon. Many a section has benefitted from the fire power produced by one of these. A real battle winner. In its sustained fire role, it had an accuracy out to 1800 meters firing 800 rounds per minute.
GUN. Term used to specify the requirement of the GPMG or Gun Group to specify the gun team.
HGV 3. Licences to drive trucks came in three types prior to the European Union standardisation. Heavy Goods Vehicle class 3 enabled you to drive a vehicle with a gross train weight of 7.5 tonnes and 2 axles with a rigid frame. An HGV 2 was the same except it was multiple axles, and finally HGV 1 was a vehicle that was articulated. There was no upper weight limit applicable to these groups. In the 1990s they became Category C which amalgamated the old HGV 3 and 2 and C+E which was the articulated. (E represented a trailer with unlimited axles)
Herforder Pils. Herforder Pils is a German Pilsener style beer brewed by Herforder Brauerei GmbH & Co. KG in Herford, Germany. Stock beer in northern BAOR for British soldiers.

Known as Herfy's and the distinctive carry out yellow box of 8 bottles known as a Herfy or yellow Handbag.
Hameln. Large city on the river Weser, famed for being home of the Pied Piper in local myth and where the Glockenspiel was first invented. Located North West of Hildesheim. Military garrison town.
HF. High frequency used in army radios. Defined as such for all frequencies between 2Khz and 29.999Khz.
HIP. A Russian built cargo or troop-carrying helicopter designated as a Mil Mi-8. It was first introduced in service since 1978.
Kartofolen (Kartofle, Kartofolen) German words for potato.
Kerrimec. A kerrimec is similar to a shipping container but made of aluminium. They are converted into accommodation, shower and toilets and even field kitchens. This can be done very quickly within a secure area.
Lederhosen. Typical Tyrolean dress consisting of bib and braces and trousers similar to plus fours. The material is usually leather or soft moleskin type cloth.
Lee Enfield .303 rifle was the standard army issue weapon from before World War 2. It was gradually phased out during the 1960 and 1970 and only remained with cadet units until the 1990s.
MOD. Ministry of Defence, based in Whitehall London.
MFO Box. Married Forces Overseas box. A collapsible but durable box made from plywood used to transport personal effects in shipping containers around bases. Designed for family use but widely abused around the army as very useful containers.
MILAN. This is the French made Missile, Light anti-tank infantry missile given its French designation. This was an anti tank wire guided missile with a range of 2km brought into service in the early 1970s to replace the WOMBAT. The TA NATO battalions received theirs in 1980. The live firing of these was closely

controlled as the missile was rumoured to cost £10k in the 1980s. Our war stocks were incredibly disproportionate to our missiles. Each firing post had four missiles allocated. A further two per post were kept at first line with a brigade controlled reserve of sixteen being pooled some ten miles from where the Soviet tanks in their hundreds would be bearing down on our positions.

MORATORIAM. The definition of this is a legally authorized period of delay in the performance of a legal obligation. This came about when the government had to save a huge proportion of the defence budget after the three-day week and the miners strikes back in the 1970s. All public services were cut back and expenditure delayed, to help the financial deficit sort itself out.

MTO's PA. Motor Transport Officers' personal assistant was a throwback to the past where officers had a batman to look after his kit and prepare his meals in the field. This role usually went to his driver and in return the driver did no duties other than to put up the command post tent and camouflage. He was widely known as a slacker mainly because he would keep himself in public view when others were digging or engaged in arduous duties. Also notorious for remaining in his sleeping bag during an attack whilst keeping his weapon in a plastic bag spotlessly clean. As the years went by it was phased out and officers looked after themselves exactly as soldiers.

NATO. North Atlantic Treaty Organisation. Formed in 1947 based in New York.

Ops Room. Operation room, where the operation is controlled.

Operation Banner. Operation Banner was the name given to the troubles in Northern Ireland. This lasted from 1969 to 1998 when the Good Friday peace agreement was brokered.

Parabellum. The 9×19mm Parabellum is a firearms cartridge that was designed by Georg Luger and introduced in 1902 by the German weapons manufacturer Deutsche Waffen und Munitions fabriken (DWM) This 9mm cartridge became the bullet and calibre of choice for most pistol and submachine manufacturers.

PSI. A permanent staff instructor, a regular soldier attached to the TA for a two-year period to standardise training and update on new methods and tactics etc. Also assists during the week to get the resources and logistics in place for evening and weekend training.

Pristina. The capital of Kosovo.

Q party. This refers to the quartermasters grouping whether the company quartermaster's sergeant or elements of B Echelon with either the QM or Technical QM.

QRF. Quick Reaction Force. This is an undefined group of soldiers who are on a moment's notice to move to deal with a situation within their specific area of operations.

RTU. Returned to unit. This was the letters of shame used when you were sent back from a course or posting with a black mark against your name.

REME. The Royal Electrical and Mechanical Engineers. These are the technical specialist who repair equipment whether it is weapons, signals equipment or vehicle related.

RQMS. Regimental quartermaster sergeant. Deputy to the Quartermaster.

Rupert's. Widely known nickname for junior inexperienced officers. Origins are unknown other than personal experience of one officer calling to another in the darkness in a tactical position.' I say Rupert where are my slippers?' whilst pronouncing the R as a W with a slight speech impediment.

SR71. The Lockheed SR71 blackbird was a very fast spy plane capable of fly on the envelope of space, developed in the 1960s by the USA. Still in service until the early 2000s.

Soviets. Shortened name for members of the United Soviet Socialist Republic.

Schleswig Holstein. An area in northern Germany formally an independent state with elements of self-governing but responsible to Bonn (West German capital pre unification).
SLR. The Self loading rifle was issued to replace the .303 from the 1960 onwards. It was a variant of the Belgian FN without the automatic capability. This had a remarkable stopping ability, using the 7.62 round. The 20-round magazine was barely able to squeeze into the 1958 pattern webbing and shut the catch.
Sennelager. Small town part of the Paderborn garrison backing onto the vast training area.
Schnell Imbiss. Translates to quick restaurant. Roadside café or mobile van serving coffee and a wide range of basic sausage, pork and chicken dishes on a paper plate or foam tray. Always has a wooden fork to consume it with.
SHAPE. Supreme Headquarters, Allied Powers in Europe.
Sibbesse gap. The valley adjacent to the small village of Sibbesse was our battalions are of operations during the cold war era. The valley would have produced an unrestricted route through the area. It is in the Hildesheim area.
Slivovitz. High octane clear spirit made from plums. Found all over the Balkans, easily distilled by the local indigenous inhabitants.
T62. The T62 battle tank was introduced into service in 1961 and followed on from the highly successful T55.
T72. The T-72 is a Soviet second-generation main battle tank that entered production in 1971. About 20,000 T-72 tanks were built, making it one of the most widely produced post–World War II tanks, second only to the T-54/55 family. The T-72 was widely exported and saw service in forty countries and in numerous conflicts.
T80. The T-80 is a third-generation main battle tank (MBT) designed and manufactured in the Soviet Union. When it entered

service in 1976, it was the first MBT in the world to feature a powerful multifuel turbine engine as its main propulsion engine.

Tachograph. A Tachograph is fitted in all commercial vehicles, both trucks over 3.5 tonnes and all coaches. These measure the driver's hours. Although we didn't have them fitted we had to adhere rigidly to the rules for rest stops and working hours laid down by the EU rules.

TEWT. Test Exercise Without Troops. This was the management practical exercises usual on a map, desk or practically out on the ground. Usually just the key commanders were involved in these as a cost reduction exercise in part.

Thetford. A market town in Norfolk. The vast training area is situated approximately 10 miles north of the town forming part of the Thetford forest, a vast wooded area owned by the forestry commission.

TA. Territorial Army was formed in 1908 as an immediate reserve in times of crisis, primarily as a home defence unit. This evolved over the years, notably in the lead up to the two world wars and through to today where the TA has evolved to the Army Reserve and is an intricate part of the British army, providing trained soldiers and small groups to support operations. From the time mentioned in the text, the TA battalions were self contained and able to deploy in support of the regular army as part of the existing brigade formations.

TURDIS. Nickname for a portable toilet shaped like the time machine in the Dr Who TV series, hence the name.

USSR. The United Soviet Socialist Republic. Amalgamation of separate states in 1922 under Joseph Stalin. Warsaw Pact countries.

Verboten. German word for forbidden.

VHF. Very High frequency used in army radios. Defined as such for all frequencies between 30 and 47 MHz in army radios.

WMD. Weapons of mass destruction. Popular phase used extensively in the Iraq war referring to the perceived threat of chemical and biological weapons.
Warrior. A Warrior is an armoured fighting vehicle under development in the 1970 for use in carrying infantry in a protected environment. The key features with this vehicle was its versatility in being able to keep up with the tanks. As they became faster and more durable, the warrior's predecessor, the AFV 432 couldn't match the capability. The warrior is fitted with a 30mm calibre chain gun capable of bringing lightly armoured vehicles to a halt.
Wehrmacht. Name for the German field army used from the early 1930s to the end of WW2.
WOMBAT 120 mm. (Weapon of Magnesium, Battalion, Anti-Tank) This was a recoil less rifle designed to take on the Soviet T64 and T72. It had a crew of four and was introduced to full service with NATO infantry battalions in the 1950s. It was a line of sight weapon, effective in its day until the French MILAN came into the order of battle. It was winched onto the back of a specially modified long wheel base land rover with the canvas top removed. These were called Portee's.
Zealand. Island part of Denmark where the capital Copenhagen is situated.
10 Para. 10th (Volunteer)Battalion the Parachute Regiment. Based in London was the second TA battalion in 6 Field force. Kitted out exactly as we were but had additional parachute capability.
4BIT. This is an ammunition term for how the rounds are loaded into the clips from the manufacturer. It stands for 4 ball rounds and then 1 tracer round. These clips could be dismantled and mixed up accordingly. Used on night shoots so the tracer can pinpoint a target for other firers.

Acknowledgements
I would like to thank my wife Sue for her patience and help with the technical stuff etc. Also, thanks to Paul Barker, Sarah Warren, Nigel Sutton, Ray and Janie Lloyd, and finally Nick Jung for taking the time to read through and sense check and provide feedback where needed.

Research sources;
Wikipedia
3 PWRR
Ordnance survey
PWRR and Queen's Museum
www.armytigers.com
Ministry of Defence
Janes Defence weekly

Disclaimer. The contents of this manuscript are entirely the memories and recollections of the author. Any research material and photographs have been acknowledged above. If any errors or omissions have been made apologies are given in advance and further revisions will reflect this and sincere apologies offered.

About the author

John Bennett was born in Canterbury and educated locally. In 1973 he joined the motor trade and trained as a mechanic. In 1978 he joined the Territorial Army partly to assist in work progression and partly through curiosity as his uncle was in the TA in 1938 through to his sad death in 1941. It was through the memories of his mother and a vast number of photographs and letters that the interest was born. In 1988 John left the motor trade and joined Sun Alliance insurance as a Staff Motor Engineer where he progressed via a convoluted route to become a team leader of motor engineers in the North of England, Scotland and Northern Ireland. John took early retirement in 2013 and is involved with the PWRR Regimental association, assisting with its growth and development. John is also passionate about the Regimental Museum in Dover Castle and works as a volunteer assisting with outreach projects and doing talks and tours. John is also on the Regimental heritage committee representing the TA and Army reserve.

Cover photographs.

Front cover – Media operations Crowborough camp pre deployment.

Rear Cover - Kazakhstan on the ranges 45c heat

Printed in Great Britain
by Amazon

38333111R00128